Gemstones From Heaven

Written by Michael C. King

God Signs Series: Book 1

Gemstones From Heaven © Copyright 2016

This book and other titles by Michael King can be found at TheKingsofEden.com

Available from Amazon.com, Createspace.com, and other retail outlets.

ISBN-13: 978-1537139562

ISBN-10: 1537139568

Printed in the USA

Table of Contents

Dedication

I dedicate this book to my wife, best friend, and life partner, Sunshine L King. I am blessed every day to wake up married to you, and I am very happy with our life together. We have had ups and downs on this journey, but without you the experiences and wisdom shared in this book would not have been possible. Thank you.

Acknowledgments

Thank you God for stunning me time and time again with these shiny, beautiful heavenly gifts. They are such tangible reminders of your inexhaustible goodness and unexplainable love, and I will thank you throughout all eternity for who you are. I love you.

A hearty thanks to my wife Sunshine King for the editing work. You have taught me a lot about *good* writing, and you always make my work better.

Special thanks to Denise Hayes for the cover design. Your skill and artistic eye with graphic design are second to none.

Thank you to Carla Reed and the ministerial-couple for introducing me to the gemstone manifestation. It holds a special place in my heart.

Praying Medic and Praying Medic's Wife, you both bless me thoroughly, and without your help this book would not be in existence. I am grateful for your friendship and love, and for the many ways you enrich my life. Thank you.

Finally, thanks to Lynn Winesett for your assistance in catching remaining typos prior to printing! It is amazing to me how we can edit a book multiple times and still miss simple mistakes—thanks for taking the time to make this book better. You are a blessing!

Preface

Dear Reader,

    As you read, it is my express hope that your life is enriched and your faith strengthened in God's ability to do far more than you can imagine. My intent in writing this book is to shed light on the gemstone manifestation and to answer the most common questions people ask about this sign from heaven. My prayer as you read this is that your heart is enriched and this gemstone sign begins to manifest and increase in your life and that the provision and favor of God floods your home.

Multiple and abundant blessings,

Michael King

Chapter 1

Our Personal Testimony

In January of 2015 (earlier this year) God told me that gemstones would begin to appear more frequently around us. I was excited, as I have seen this manifestation hundreds of times before in the past few years. More recently gems appeared very infrequently, and for a few reasons. Before going further, however, some of you readers may not have heard of this before, so let me explain.

In the early spring of 2012 a friend of mine, Carla, came for a visit. She is a musician and sound therapist; when she passes through Portland every so often, we and some other friends make sure to visit her. This particular visit she had a surprise for all of us, but we didn't know the half of it.

We went to a retired chiropractor's house to meet some other friends of hers who had come for a visit. All together there were nine of us present at this gathering. One couple had a unique manifestation of the Lord happen around them, something that had been going on for five years at that time—

namely that gemstones from heaven would literally appear around them, both on the ground and in the air.

The stones themselves all have brilliant facets. Some of the facets are cut so strangely that it flabbergasts jewelers because people simply do not make jewelry this way. For example, I have a gem that is an irregular, rhomboidal shape. Out of the thousands I have seen appear, I have only once seen a raw, rough, uncut stone. The majority are amethysts, peridot, emerald, garnets, and rubies, along with an occasional aquamarine. There are also clear and yellow stones, probably different colors of topaz.

In all honesty, I cannot tell for certain what any of these stones are since I've never had any professionally tested, but some are pretty obvious just by looking at them. Since this started, I bought a diamond-tester. Very few of the ones I have found are diamonds, suggesting the clear and yellow ones are topaz or some other stone. Most of the gemstones are the size of the head of an eraser, and the teeny tiny ones are actually as uncommon as really large ones.

Each stone is unique, but some stand out more than others. On rare occasion there will be a mystic fire topaz, a stone that has three colors in it that are all mixed together. They are some of my favorites. Carnelian, an orange stone, rarely appear as well, and are a unique change when they do. My stepdaughter found a stone once that had streaks of gold in it, and she also found a raw stone once—the only uncut stone I have ever seen appear. Occasionally a larger jewel will show up including ones that are the size of a fingernail or larger. Rarer still, probably close to one in five-thousand gems or more, will be a stone that appears in a setting of some kind. This can be in a ring, cuff links, pendant, or earrings. On at least one occasion that I know of, the chain even appeared with the pendant!! In addition to all of these stones, from time to time a feather, usually at least an inch or two long, would appear in midair near one man. It was almost as if he was fluffing wings and stray feathers were falling off.

Sometimes the gems will grow in size; they can be prayed for when chipped and heal, even multiply! One of our grandchildren put one in a box once, and when she opened the box again, a second smaller one that was otherwise identical was sitting next to it. The gem had a baby!

Sunshine, my wife, and I were like little children that first evening, running around and picking up gemstones off of the floor. Sometimes we would hear them fall out of midair and land on the hardwood floors, sounding like a muted version of a rain stick—the wooden musical devices filled with beans or seeds to make rattling noises.

Other times we simply found them on the surfaces where they appeared, such as on a coffee table or windowsill. At one point we laid down on the floor in the middle of the foyer and I asked God to hit us with gems. I remember having my eyes closed and feeling something hit my shoulder then heard the sound of rattling across the floor. We both shouted with great delight, and I can still remember my wife's excitement as she went around picking them up. She is so child-like when they fall. To this day she still squeals with joy every time she finds one, and I have to imagine God loves that.

That first weekend my wife and I experienced this manifestation was a whirlwind. We spent that Friday night in an evening of worship, fellowship, laughter, and gemstone-hunting throughout the house. Carla is a pianist and led us in some worship songs on the Baby Grand piano in the chiropractor's living room. We took communion in an "upper room," i.e. one of the upstairs bedrooms, and as a whole, God just rocked our night.

Saturday was a bit of a mental break, as our minds attempted to process the absolutely amazing experiences we had the night before. Although "break" is sort of a relative term. I must have called at least four friends and told them all about our experience and what God had been doing.

Sunday was a blast. We went to church and shared with a bunch of people what we had experienced. That evening we went to another meeting that ministry couple held at a church on the other side of the city. That night was really fun too, because not only did we have our new friends there, but a pair of our long-time friends, Hope and Beth, drove several hours to reach the gathering. Hope and Beth are precious women and are both what I refer to as God-junkies—they will go anywhere and do almost anything if God is in it. When we told them about the gems, their response was, "Where do we need to be and when?"

We spent Sunday evening listening to the husband, whom the manifestation seemed to center around, share about his life journey and how God brought him salvation as well as this unique gem miracle years later. The people at that church were very kind, and so many people wanted to share the gems to make sure everyone had at least one. It was like a room full of starving people, but each one made sure the other had a piece of bread before they were content to eat their own. This meeting showed me how hungry people are to see God work miraculously in their lives. We *all* desire a visible demonstration of the invisible God, and even more, a tangible demonstration of His love for us.

For myself, the mind-blowing experience just continued. I felt *so* incredibly loved by my Heavenly Father, who loved me so much that he would not only obliterate my experience of "impossible," but do it with such beautiful and valuable items. I mean, how many other gods have we ever heard of that hand out gemstones to their followers?

A year or so later, we invited the couple with the gems to hold a Gem Party at our house—a twelve-hour revolving door of fellowship, food, and fun. During the day we had a very informal hang-out, and people of all ages were literally crawling on our carpet picking up stones. In the evening we had a more focused time of worship and the man shared his testimony, similar to the one I heard a year prior.

At that time they brought out some of the more spectacular gemstones God has given them. Many of these are large, and by large I mean the size of a quarter or larger. From talking to friends, counting my own bag of gems, and observing the gems others picked up, I estimated that over four-thousand gems appeared in that twelve hours.

I will be honest; I consider this a conservative estimate, based on the number of people present and the quantity of gems each of them left with, and I suspect the number approaches six-thousand. At the end of that meeting, I had over one-hundred gems myself; that didn't include the massive amount my wife, stepdaughter, her husband and my grandkids each had, or the stashes that the other twenty-six people who came left with by the end of the day. Some people left with far more than I did!

This meeting sparked something, and we held one every two to three months for the rest of that year. Not only that, but it turned into a series of meetings throughout the surrounding area. Gem Parties have been held at four or more different people's houses since then, the most recent one happened almost a year and a half after we stopped holding meetings at our house.

Fast forward again to January of this year (2015), three years after we first experienced the gem manifestation and a year after we stopped having meetings, we still had gems show up but it was usually one gem with a four-month interval in-between. I prayed and talked to God about this and reminded Him that His Word says when we honor someone we can have their reward. I repented for any ways we had been dishonoring to the gem-ministers (as all relationships have conflicts and this was no different), and asked God to fix anything that was hindering the flow of gems in our lives. Shortly thereafter, God told me that gems would begin to appear again and with greater frequency. When he told me this I was excited, but also somewhat reserved. After all, a single stone every month would be more frequent than what we had experienced the previous year prior, and God has a way of doing things very differently than what we imagine it will look like.

To my amazement, on January 31, within a week and a half of God telling me the gems would increase, I found the first stone. It was a clear white color and conspicuously perched on the edge of my granddaughter's bed. She had fallen asleep in our bed and I was taking her downstairs at midnight to tuck her into her own. As I drew near to the bed and saw it, I immediately recognized the gem for what it was. I showed my wife, who, yet again, squealed with delight.

The next one appeared on my stepdaughter's wedding day on our back patio—a wedding gift from our Heavenly Father. On Saturday, May 23, we had a gem-breakout while we were replacing our dining room carpet with flooring. Since we were pulling up the carpet, I told everyone to be on the lookout for gems in case any had appeared *under* the carpet when we held the Gem Parties years before. Sure enough, my stepdaughter found one while I was out at Home Depot. Go figure.

Something in this process, whether our faith and expectation or something else entirely, sparked a supernatural whirlwind. For the rest of that weekend, into the next week and for weeks afterward, gems appeared. They started by simply showing up on the floor and on the window ledges, but after a few hours advanced to falling out of midair onto the new flooring. In fact, it became so prolific and distracting that it took us two days to complete what would have been a one-day project, but God wasn't done. To date, we had never seen a blue sapphire appear, and we had a handful of them appear that weekend!

While that may not seem significant to some, blue sapphires hold special significance to my wife and me in regards to our marriage. Blue sapphires are an older tradition than diamonds for marriage. Sunshine's nickname for her unknown "man-to-be" even before we ever met was Blue Sapphire. Once, before we were even seeing each other much less got married, she was wearing a blue sapphire ring and I prophesied over it. I also had a blue sapphire ring on my wedding finger in the spirit realm which God had given me years before we met. When blue sapphires began to appear it felt like God had taken this now-familiar manifestation to an even deeper place of love and meaning for us.

At the writing of this book we have not yet had any more gemstone-whirlwinds, but gems have continued to steadily appear around us, and I am encouraged that God is releasing this manifestation to the earth at a new level. Two years ago was the seventh-year anniversary for the gem manifestation starting, and we have now entered into the second seven-year cycle. It feels to me like we are part of a second-generation of this manifestation, where God is opening up new and exciting things and the circle of glory is spreading out even wider into the earth.

Chapter 2

What Does This Mean?

Over the years I have had experiences that caused me to hunger to know God more. I have seen the miraculous and heard the stories. Starting at childhood, this has grown over the years. I went to this meeting, which I attend regularly, with a desire to see another stone manifest from God's world to ours to give to a friend of mine on Facebook who lives in another country. He reads stories and follows some of the churches that have signs and wonders, but said there are none near him, so he asked me to send him one if they appeared. These signs cannot be produced; they are strictly the love of God manifesting to us. Like Jesus told the scribes (religious), who hated the fact that he forgave the paralytic man his sins, "Which is harder, to say his sins are forgiven, or rise up and walk? Then he told the man, rise up and walk, and he gained strength in his legs and rose up and walked." Mark 2:1-12

Well, if God can manifest his presence in our meetings, why not send a gift from his realm to ours? It happens. Anyway, I have seen others find stones and heard friends tell me stories of how their stones came to them, all second hand to me, but I believed them because I have known some of these people for 30 years. I too have had some wonderful encounters with the living God! But this time, it happened to me. We were taking communion and I reached to the tray to grab my little glass of wine (which also comes directly from the throne room) and could clearly see through the glasses all sitting there together, because the wine was not dark, the room was well lit, and the disposable wine cups were clear plastic. I was careful to lift a glass from the tray and bring it to my lap without spilling any wine. As my hand went to grab the glass, I felt a sensation come on it and didn't think too much about it . . . but I got this feeling to look at my glass again, so I glanced down, and thought I saw a dark spot, so I tilted my glass to get a better look, and saw the spot was even more defined so I took that glass and shot it up to the light from the lamp. Bam! I have a stone, I have a stone!

I could not wait to take communion, to drink the wine in remembrance of Him, so I could see what color and shape my stone was. I was dumbfounded and in awe. My stone was a purple heart—a deep purple heart! I told everyone that I had a stone and we all rejoiced together. My husband was sitting right beside me and said that he had a revelation about it and wanted to tell me. That is too much to write here, but two other people came up to me to specifically to tell me that the stone represented so much more than I even knew right off the bat, and God was going to download this revelation to me. I am so excited to say I can hardly wait to know more! That is why I am not ashamed of the gospel, and never will be. I have relationship, not religion, supernatural, not ritualistic. The church is not my source, God is. He has been there since my birth, and deep calls unto deep. If you are hungry, go seeking. Don't blame the church for not teaching you what you could seek out on your own. God is able and willing; He is just amazing! I will never be the same, and I am starving to know my Father more! His love compels me.

Later, I began to understand the meaning of the purple heart; that Jesus calls some to the chamber with Him and praying as one united in his tears, we target what his heart wants to intercede for. That could be individuals or nations. As the Purple Heart implies, "knowing intimately and experientially" the wounds of others, we release people from the things that crushed them and left them unable to correctly discern His love for them darkening their own value. We breathe life afresh into them. They come in all colors, from every nation. We may bundle them together in one supernatural life bubble and blow into it until life force intervention has once again preserved their existence and has strengthened them to press on until, by faith, the next rescue finds them in the presence of men or Angels. It is in fullness His Purple Heart.

Kathy Allen

****

Since we began to experience the gems, many have asked us what these gemstones mean and what God is saying and doing. I have my own thoughts and opinions, which are by no means the "certified" correct answer, but I do believe I can offer insight into a portion of what God is saying and doing. To begin with, I believe this particular miracle is a bit hard to classify. For example, is it a sign, a wonder, or a miracle? While I suggest that the gem-couple mentioned in the last chapter, and specifically the husband operates in a gift of miraculous powers for gemstone apportation, and those around him seem to have it rub off on them, it doesn't follow the same controllable pattern that many other spiritual gifts follow.

Tongues, interpretation of tongues, prophecy, gifts of healings, words of knowledge, words of wisdom, and discernment of spirits can all be engaged to some great extent at-will of the user, and I am a firm believer that if most of the gifts can be used that way, all of the gifts can be used that way. Over the past few years I have explored the means by which we engage those other gifts to understand how one might purposefully engage miraculous powers, and more specifically gemstone miracles. I have found that there seems to be little relationship between the appearance of gemstones and our human activity. Gems appear quite often when we least expect them, not when we are most focused on finding them, although they can appear then too. As such, it is hard to narrowly define their appearances as a miracle although it certainly falls well within the confines of that category. On the other hand, I suggest it is simultaneously a sign and a wonder as well. A sign is pretty straightforward, being an event or action that points to something else, and the gemstones definitely do that. A wonder is harder to describe but seems to be closely aligned with an action or event that causes us to be more in awe of God.

I believe this gem-sign points to a number of things. In ancient Jewish culture, the father of the groom was the one who decided whether the groom was ready to marry his betrothed or not. The groom was required to add a room onto the family house and had to adorn it with sufficient comforts to ensure the wife would be comfortable in her future dwelling. Once the bridegroom's father felt the groom had sufficiently prepared a place for her, the groom would then go and bring his bride to be with him there. Jesus spoke of this reality in John 14:2-3 where he said, "My Father's house has many rooms; if that were not so, would I have told you that I am going there to prepare a place for you? And if I go and prepare a place for you, I will come back and take you to be with me that you also may be where I am. (NIV)" This statement of his wasn't random and out of context. Instead, his disciples understood he was speaking of them as being as important to him as a bride. In ancient Jewish culture, when the bridegroom came to collect his bride, he would adorn her with jewels then take her to his father's house to be with her forever. In the same way, God is adorning us with gems and even settings of gold and silver before bringing us to be with Him. Additional references about God giving jewels to His people, His Bride, are as follows: Genesis 24:53, Isaiah 54:11-15, Isaiah 61:10, Jeremiah 2:32, Ezekiel 16:9-14, Zechariah 9:16.

To take this idea one step further, God is not just Jesus' father, but He is our heavenly Father as well. It was customary in the Middle East, and still happens to this day in some places where women are still regarded as little more than possessions, that the father of the bride was required to provide a dowry, essentially a payment from the bride's family to the groom's. Although God regards us as far more valuable than possessions, in keeping with ancient customs God is sending us literal physical gemstones that we will carry with us into this spiritual marriage with Jesus, our bridegroom.

The second message I see God sharing with us is one of joy. We are His children, and we must become like children to enter the Kingdom of Heaven. Kids have one main job in life and that is to play! Our Father delights in us, his children. Psalm 16:11 says, "You make known to me the path of life; you will fill me with joy in your presence, with eternal pleasures at your right hand (NIV). It is an absurd notion if we believe God doesn't want us to have fun. One of the main objections I have witnessed to this manifestation is that of the staunchly religious and otherwise stuck-in-the-mud people who seem to forget that God started the book of Genesis by placing his new creations in a garden full of delights in a land titled Pleasure (Eden). God is possibly the most hedonistic being of the universe, and He wants us to share in his limitless joy! Why send us gems? Why NOT send us gems? They are so incredibly fun!

The third thing I see God doing is found in 1 Corinthians 2:9, "However, as it is written: "What no eye has seen, what no ear has heard, and what no human mind has conceived" the things God has prepared for those who love him." God is able to do far more than we can imagine in our human minds and human thinking, so much so that we've never even heard of many of the spectacular things God has planned for us.

In Isaiah 558-9 God says, "'For my thoughts are not your thoughts, neither are your ways my ways,' declares the Lord. 'As the heavens are higher than the earth, so are my ways higher than your ways and my thoughts than your thoughts.'" God is interested in raising our faith. God wants us to have the opportunity to ask and believe for far more than we have ever asked before, and what better way to do that than completely wreck our beliefs and understanding of what He will and won't do for us.

Fourth, I see this as a manifestation of provision. When we see gems appear, along with the feathers and gold dust I mentioned prior, how can it do anything but raise our belief in a Divine Provider? There is a church in Puerto Rico that had a significant gem manifestation a number of years back (I am unsure if it is still happening today), and they were able to sell gems which allowed them to finance God's work in their area. I have heard other stories that I cannot confirm where other churches had so much gold dust appear that they were able to pay off and/or fund a building program off the proceeds from the gold sales. Who needs man's provision when God shows up? My wife's family were close friends with two missionary women who often had money and train tickets appear in their pockets, and food was supernaturally provided for them. God is our provider, and while oftentimes He uses other people to supply all our needs and wants, He doesn't have to wait helplessly in heaven in hopes that humans will heed his requests. He can create new things as easily as He did when he created the heavens and the earth!

Fifth, this sign is a witness to all of God's hand at work. In other words, it's a sign that points directly to Him. I have shared gems with countless people, and many have come up with their own names and explanations for what they are and how they appear, but the message I give is always consistent and always points to Him. It is not uncommon for me to hear someone ask me about my "fairy gems" or "magic gems," and while some might get upset about applying New Age language to God's gifts, I don't. They may use different terminology, but they recognize that God is up to something and they are simply speaking out of their own grid of understanding.

The sixth thing I see God doing with the gems is something that a friend shared with me a while back. She said, "We have had gems tested, and when different people brought the same gem into the same jeweler, he got different results based on what the person who brought the stone in believed about the stone." Entire churches get in a theological uproar over whether the gems are or aren't from God, and although many churches at first received the manifestation with joy, they later rejected the gems due to the controversy inside that fellowship afterwards. One thing my friend Carla shared with me once has always stuck with me: "God told us once that people think they are testing the gems, but in reality the gems are testing them."

In the week prior to our first Gem Party there was definitely a question that went through our household of "What if no gems show up?" The gems test all of us in a number of ways, including whether God will show up, whether we need to "help God along" by planting gems, and they test our ideas of what God can and cannot do, as well as how much we are willing to let God be God and do what He wants to do. I believe God uses the gemstones and other supernatural manifestations as a plumb line for our hearts. Are we a people who are hungry for God and his ways and ready to embrace the new things He is revealing to us, or are we so suspicious, jaded, and cynical that anything we see gets put through a spiritual spectrometer to thoroughly test and understand every aspect before we can receive it with joy?

Many people have asked me if I have ever had my gems tested. No. Honestly, I've never felt the need to do so to prove the gems are real. I can figure out what stones they most likely are just by looking at them, and the only testing I have ever tried is to see if the clear ones were diamonds or not. Other than that, it just doesn't matter to me, not to mention that testing gems can get really expensive very quickly, especially when you have hundreds of them. Whether they are glass or crystal I find to be of no real significance in that these are tangible reminders of God's love toward me. The material they are made of doesn't in any way alter the fact that these stones appeared from the heaven-dimension, some of which fell from midair in my living room!

Gemstones From Heaven

Sometimes I think God does things just because He can, and sometimes there are so many reasons behind His actions that we can only begin to touch the surface of what He is doing. For example, some of the gems had cracks in them when they appeared, and others chipped or cracked sometime after they manifested on earth. I had one that was completely whole when I placed it in a plastic bag, and later when I looked at it, the stone was chipped, but no chip was floating around in the bag with it. The chipped-off part had literally vanished into thin air! It seems completely absurd to me that God would send us gems from heaven that are flawed, but then, aren't we all cracked or blemished in some ways? Doesn't God send us as untarnished spirits into the earth where we then pick up cracks and chips on our journey through life? People have actually prayed for "injured" gems and they have recovered. I believe this is just one more layer of the depths of the things God is doing in and through the gems—that we, too, can be healed just as the gems can. Sometimes, too, the cracks will form pictures. I have a suspicion that some of these gems have a mission of their own when they arrive on earth, and that they form cracks and chips because their heavenly energy is being released into the earth and they literally become smaller or less perfect as a result.

In addition to releasing glory in the earth, gems appear to act as a sort of spiritual barometer. Revival Magazine is an online publication from Catch The Fire Network, birthed out of the Toronto Outpouring in 1994. This magazine featured an article in December of 2013 that speaks of Life Foundation

Center, an orphanage and ministry in Jeuura, Orissa, India. The children at the center have been having unique visitations from Jesus over the past years and, during worship, have been taken into the heavens on a regular basis to be trained for spiritual warfare in the region. They have also been having gemstones appear. The article says this: "The stones from heaven appeared in their hands and on the floor. We could see in their hand movements that they were receiving large stones but the specimens that they picked up were often very tiny. We asked them why the stones are so tiny. Jesus said to them, 'The size of the stones that appear on earth determines the density of the spiritual darkness of the territory (Fernando)'".

It would appear that the gemstones themselves are a shadow of a heavenly reality, and that while they do appear on earth, if the earth begins to look more like heaven, the size of the gems that appear might begin to grow. Likewise, it is also possible that in areas of great spiritual darkness that the gems might appear much smaller, or even less frequently. Keep in mind that this is not an absolute. If tiny gems begin to appear in your home where there were no gems before, don't automatically assume God is telling you how spiritually dark your home is, but be open to the idea that there may be areas for growth as well.

One of my main motivating factors for holding our gem parties was a belief I still hold today. I firmly believe we need to have encounters with God that expand our view of what is possible. In a world that is full of anger, violence, depression, sickness, and poverty, we need a higher perspective. When natural, economic, or even emotional disasters threaten our way of life, we must have a deep reservoir of experiences in and with God that stabilize us in those troubled times. It was my heart's desire to create a space where people could experience this life-altering miracle, and in so-doing reach a new level of understanding of who God is and what He is like.

My own life has been so radically altered by the things I have experienced, including but not limited to gold dust, feathers, and gemstones appearing and sometimes even disappearing again, objects supernaturally sticking to walls, as well as a variety of other strange and wonderful spiritual encounters. God is so much greater than we can ask or think of, and He is interested in taking us deep into His realms of glory and mystery if we will open ourselves up to new things. This manifestation is not limited to what I have shared here as God always has deeper purposes behind what He is doing than what we are able to understand, but I believe gems from heaven are giving us a small glimpse into His higher plans and purposes.

Chapter 3

Deception and Discernment

Interesting night tonight. Spent a lovely evening sharing dinner, sharing testimonies, blessing one couple among us, and God dropped gems all over the carpet. Together, we probably gathered 60 or 80 small ones (jewelry size) just tonight. I stood back, aloof, for a while. "We must honor the Gift-Giver more than pursue the gifts!" I (a little self-righteously) told myself.

Father chuckled at me. "If you gave your children a good gift, and they pushed it aside and just sat there, staring at you, would you really love that? When you give a gift, you want it to be appreciated. You want to make them happy. How do you think I feel?" So I gathered 8 or 10 little ones. I watched some of them appear right in front of my eyes. And you know, it really did make me happy. We have such an awesome Dad. And as a bride, we have an awesome groom, and a pretty epic future father-in-law."

Northwest Prophetic

****

I was in a meeting a while back where I found 2 of 3 gems. The two I found appeared right before my eyes. I was looking and then blinked and looked and there were those two gems with a few others. No one threw gems, they were just "there" and I was rather greedy and grabbed for two. Another one was given to me by someone walking by me as I sat on the steps and it was sitting right next to me. Whether gems appear or not doesn't affect my salvation one way or the other—I am saved because I believe in Jesus and He is God's only begotten Son and He died for ALL my sins. I accept what He did for me and have entered into covenant with him almost 39 years ago—finding gemstones was like icing on an already yummy cake.

I know the devil didn't throw these gems and I know no human threw these gems, and I am grateful to my Papa God for blessing me with these 'trinkets' from another dimension parallel to this one. I give you glory Jesus, and I do not in any way elevate anyone else to this place of worship and praise. God is able to do exceeding abundantly above ALL we can ask, think, or believe—He is God! I am a "son/daughter of God" and highly cherished and beloved!

Jule Wolfe

****

It is impossible to fully discuss supernatural events if we didn't address the D-word: Deception. So many people get worried and worked up about getting deceived over a manifestation such as this one, and while it is good to walk in wisdom, I think it is often much simpler than people make it. The two methods the Bible gives for testing something over time are a spiritual gift of discernment and testing the fruit of the people involved.

The biggest complaint, and actually the only complaint I have ever heard about the gems, is that some believe this is the work of the devil and not God. Dissenters have a limited few reasons why they believe this is so, namely that "God doesn't do that," that the gems are a distraction from God, and that they draw people away from the Gospel. Personally, I find these objections a bit ridiculous. Usually those who claim it is demonic have never experienced the manifestation and simply bristle at the idea of God making cut gems appear in our midst. Mind you, these same people ardently believe that God made manna appear six of every seven days for forty years for the Israelites, but when gems appear on occasion for us, not even daily, it's the work of the devil. That alone should make anyone pause to reconsider his perspective, but we can feel confident this is God at work for several other reasons.

First, the Bible is full of verses about gems. If we want to say this is a demonic manifestation, what do we do about those verses that point to it being from God? There are a number of verses where God states that He will give His people gems of varying kinds, listed below. (Keep in mind that Jerusalem is both an actual place and a prophetic picture of the Bride of Christ, the people of God.)

Isaiah 45:3 "I will give you hidden treasures, riches stored in secret places, so that you may know that I am the LORD, the God of Israel, who summons you by name."

Isaiah 54:11-13 "Afflicted city, lashed by storms and not comforted, I will rebuild you with stones of turquoise, your foundations with lapis lazuli. I will make your battlements of rubies, your gates of sparkling jewels, and all your walls of precious stones. All your children will be taught by the LORD, and great will be their peace.

Ezekiel 16:11-14 "I adorned you with jewelry: I put bracelets on your arms and a necklace around your neck, and I put a ring on your nose, earrings on your ears and a beautiful crown on your head. So you were adorned with gold and silver; your clothes were of fine linen and costly fabric and embroidered cloth. Your food was honey, olive oil and the finest flour. You became very beautiful and rose to be a queen. And your fame spread among the nations on account of your beauty, because the splendor I had given you made your beauty perfect, declares the Sovereign LORD."

Next, the complaint comes that the devil is distracting us by taking our focus off of God. Funny, but between the ten or more gatherings I have held and been a part of, all of them were all about God and His goodness! In theory, if the enemy was going to deceive people, shouldn't there be some way they are being drawn away from God? Instead, what I have observed is that people feel how much more God loves them when the gems appear. Plus, their faith level in God's ability to provide increases. The devil has been around for thousands of years. He may be evil, but he isn't stupid. If we were to constantly praise God for these supposed works of the devil's, and if they actually were from the devil, he would eventually stop doing them and find a way to deceive us that was actually effective.

The third reason people tend to cite the gems being a demonic manifestation is that it draws people away from the gospel. I'm sorry, but this argument doesn't hold water either. One of the things I have personally observed when people see the gems manifest is that their excitement about sharing the good news of Jesus Christ with friends and family increases. In fact, the gems have become an evangelistic tool. Some of the jewelry I have worn that is made from the heavenly gemstones have been great conversation starters about God, and it opens up discussion about God's power to heal and do miracles today. The gospel of Jesus Christ involves the fact that we are not just saved from sin, but that Jesus heals our diseases and sickness, provides hope in our problems, and provides in our times of need. Jesus himself said it best in John 10:10b "I am come that they might have life, and that they might have it more abundantly (Blue Red and Gold Bible)." The gospel is far more broad-reaching than the narrow traditional view that has been taught in most of the

Church, one that said Jesus came to save us from our sins and that was all.

It is my opinion that if someone wants to claim this is a demonic deception then they must have an intelligent response for all of the items I have mentioned above, and I will be honest, unless they have personally been part of this gemstone experience, it will be impossible to do anything other than refute things based on their ideology and theological views without actually taking into account the real-life facts. In the end, I really don't think people need to get worked up about "deception" with this manifestation.

I think it is important to point out and remember that discernment is an inner perception, not a hard scriptural fact. In other words, it is not as easy as pointing to a single verse that we believe clearly outlines a scriptural truth, then leveling the "heresy finger" at the opponent. We all interpret scriptures differently. Just recently, my wife was at a local church meeting where the pastor spent over an hour preaching about the woes of certain "deceived, maverick Christians" whereas my wife spent the entire service grieving in her heart over the serious error in what this pastor shared. If I had been there I might not have been as kind as my wife, who simply sat there next to tears.

Each of us has to look at the manifestation individually, consider the change it brings in our own hearts, and test the results. I can honestly say that I believe this manifestation has made me a better person and a stronger believer, one who dares to expect even more for this miraculous Kingdom of Heaven to manifest on the earth. I have gone through struggles and areas of growth during the meetings we have held, but all of these things speak to me of the refining nature of God's hand at work in my life, much like cutting and polishing a rough gem so that it sparkles even more brilliantly. Have there been conflicts in my own household and with friends over this? Yes. Am I happy about those conflicts and the results? No. Do I believe this means God isn't in it? No. Our responses to what God does in no way legitimizes OR denigrates what God is doing, but over time the fruit of God's work will be life-giving. Even with those conflicts I have had, I am not remotely sorry for the gem experiences or for those who introduced me to them, and if I had the option of the experiences with the conflicts or no gems and no problems, I would choose the former every time.

The fruit I have seen in my own life and in that of others is that people fall more in love with God. We are more blessed at the end of the day than at the beginning. People have had their hearts touched by the gem manifestation in ways that have absolutely nothing to do with gems at all, but those gems acted as a confirmation from Heaven in regards to other things God was saying and doing in that person's heart. Inner healing has occurred during these gem parties as well.

In May of this year, when this gem-storm occurred at our house, my eldest granddaughter, who is seven, was crying and quite upset that God wouldn't give her a big rainbow-colored stone like she had asked Him. She didn't understand why God wouldn't do what she was asking and was feeling unloved by Him, the exact opposite of the purpose of the gems. I had to take her aside and help her calm down, then we sat on her bed and had a short discussion about gratitude and appreciating what God was doing while still asking Him for what she wanted. She left her room feeling much better and continued to play and enjoy the gems. Not twenty minutes later, while we were laying more flooring, she came running back out of her room yelling. "God did it! He gave me my stone! Look everyone! Look!" She was holding a clear stone that was the size of a quarter. It was beautifully cut and had 57 facets to it. Not only that, but I held it up to the sunlight and it cast rainbows on the wall. Yes, God had given her a large rainbow-stone. When I use wisdom and discernment about this event, I have no problem saying that yes, this was God at work. Even now as I write this, it brings me to tears as I am brought more in touch with God's love for his children, and for my grandchildren. He is so incredibly kind and generous and loving, far more than I could ever claim to be.

While this was happening, and even while I was having this discussion with my granddaughter about gems and gratitude, I was struggling in my own heart about wanting a blue sapphire ring that I wanted to give to my wife. It was somewhat important to me, and even though I was echoing the things I had said to my granddaughter in my own heart and mind, I was still struggling. A few hours later, God gave me the most beautiful, round, blue sapphire stone I think I have ever seen. It was the perfect size and shade, a deep yet brilliant blue. Yet again, God was revealing His heart of love based on what He knows is my heart's desire.

As I have already shared in this chapter, deception and discernment are not always black-and-white or cut-and-dried. This past year my wife and I were visiting a friend's church, after which they held a church-wide potluck, which we joined in on. I was telling some acquaintances we had met at another event about the gems and feathers and other supernatural manifestations we had seen. Shortly thereafter, I was walking to the food table and saw a gem sparkle on the ground. I picked it up, quite excited, and showed the friends and my wife. I walked back toward the food table and found another one! My wife directed me to look under the chairs next to me and there were almost a dozen more beneath this row of chairs! I quickly picked them up, delighted. After all, what were the chances? Fast forward an hour later and I realized that these gems appeared to be low quality and were actually a bit lighter than the gems I was used to feeling. Turns out they were plastic. Ugh! Disappointing, and not only that but I had given some to our friends as well. I was struggling with this a bit, as I don't want to be someone who is faking things or spreading hope and excitement when it's not real. I prayed about it and discussed it with my wife, as I felt that if it was indeed fake, then the appropriate thing to do would be call my friends and explain how I was mistaken. However, my wife reminded me that regardless of what they were made of, they still appeared out of nowhere, only to have ME of all people find them. I was probably one of two people in that room who expects gems to appear, the other being my wife.

The coincidence of that was just too uncanny for there not to be something more behind this. Was I deceived? Did I lead others into deception? That's a matter of personal judgment. I eventually settled on the fact that regardless of what material they are made of, they appeared. I saw it; my wife saw it. I cannot help that God chooses to do things that confound me. Why not just use real gems? I have no idea. Maybe there was some sort of growth-test for me that God was doing, but in the midst of it all, whether plastic or stone, God made them appear. This didn't remove any legitimacy from the manifestation, but rather made me evaluate on a deeper level what I believed about the gems. Is God allowed to make them out of glass, plastic, or some other substance far less valuable than diamonds? If God did nothing but rain plastic gems, would that be enough, or was my heart too hardened by my perception?

The final concern that some have had with this manifestation, and this is a concern that I believe is quite valid, is the issue of planting gems. There are two ministers that I know offhand who have been caught planting gems prior to holding a meeting. In both instances this was not swept under the rug but was quickly addressed by other church leaders. In one of the two instances, a number of churches, both from the local area and internationally, got involved and addressed the pastor in question. To the best of anyone's knowledge, in both instances the parties in question stopped doing it. And while it doesn't change the fact that people were planting gems, to the best of my knowledge all of the gems these two ministers had planted actually appeared from heaven, rather sometime prior to the meetings where they were planted.

While this is something to be aware of, this isn't something we need to overreact to. We all have places to grow in our own lives, and we are certainly not qualified to be the ones to throw the first stone. I can only hope that if I were ever in the same position as some of these ministers, with intense outside pressure from other ministers and congregants to produce miracle manifestations, that I would stay the course. I do not presume for a moment that I am somehow exempt from the same human failings that others before me have faced, and in no way do I wish to dishonor them in their struggles as each of us has our own moments of weakness.

In my own gem meetings, I confess that I watched somewhat closely to see if gems were being dropped out of a pants-leg of the ministers present or through some other method, as a local pastor I have spoken with claimed this happened in his meetings. Not only can I say I never saw this happen, but I can go a step further—when I saw the gems appear near the minister, they were often falling from about an inch or two above the carpet about two or more feet *behind* him as he walked. I can understand how some might believe he was dropping gems from his pants when they saw gems appear behind him, but the Bible does say, "These signs will follow those who believe," and follow him they do.

While many may question how and where these gems come from, and events such as gem-planting certainly do not advance anyone's faith, I cannot help but be convinced that this manifestation is clearly and only the work of our Heavenly Father of Lights in whom there is no darkness at all. Whether these gems appear from heaven, or if God is bringing us the wealth of the wicked, plundering stores of treasure sunk at the bottom of the ocean or hidden in secret vaults around the world, I truly cannot say for certain. One thing is clear to me in the midst of this unique demonstration of God's grace, is that that we are only brushing the very faintest edge of His goodness. God has far more good things stored up and planned for us than we could ask or imagine in a million years. He will freely give us all things in Jesus Christ.

Chapter 4

The Price of a Stone

A friend had gone to this conference and told me that there were gems, gold leaf, manna seeds appearing, water turning to wine was happening etc. I went on the last day and privately and silently asked the Lord if one of these gems would manifest for me. I would love one to be the color of His eyes.

I went and during the meeting a lady came up to me. She had been drinking her water bottle and said a gem appeared in the bottle. She talked to me about Jesus' DNA running through her and when she drinks the water a lot of times gems appear in the water bottle.

She handed me this beautiful stone and said she wanted to take a look at it. Then after looking at it she said, "Oh this is His eye, this color is the apple of His eye!" I was wrecked—not only because of my private chat with Jesus about the type of stone I was hoping for (if He wanted to manifest one to me), but in times past, He has talked to me about how I am the apple of His eye!

Gemstones From Heaven

For her to randomly come up to me and give me that stone and for the message of the color, it completely amazed me—that was God! Only He knew my heart and how this would impact me.

Cameo McCandless

****

When gemstones appear in your living room, or on your bed, or on the top of your head, one of the natural questions that comes to mind is, "What is this stone worth and how much can I sell this for?" The possible answers to this question can create significant controversy as opinions differ greatly from person to person. One person believes that the gems are special gifts from God and therefore should be treasured like one might treasure a gift from a close friend or spouse. This means they cannot be sold or even given to others. Another believes that the gems are given for practical reasons, to sell and pay off debt, give to a worthy cause, or even just to do something fun as a gift from God. Yet a third person believes they can be given away to friends and family and do not have to be kept personally, but that selling a gift from God would be wrong or immoral in some way.

Opinions vary, and I suggest that no one person is actually wrong but that each must act in faith as she or he feels led. 1 Corinthians 8:7-11 addresses this matter:

> "But not everyone possesses this knowledge. Some people are still so accustomed to idols that when they

eat sacrificial food they think of it as having been sacrificed to a god, and since their conscience is weak, it is defiled. But food does not bring us near to God; we are no worse if we do not eat, and no better if we do. Be careful, however, that the exercise of your rights does not become a stumbling block to the weak. For if someone with a weak conscience sees you, with all your knowledge, eating in an idol's temple, won't that person be emboldened to eat what is sacrificed to idols? So this weak brother or sister, for whom Christ died, is destroyed by your knowledge."

The underlying principle this verse addresses can be applied to the issue of selling gemstones. Some feel it is abhorrent to sell them whereas others realize we are free in Christ to keep them or sell them either way. For the one, selling the stones is a stumbling block, for the other a simple matter of course. Regardless of whether the stones are sold, each of us must be true to our own conscience. If I believe that selling them is a bad thing to do, then I should not sell them. If, however, a friend believes otherwise then that is okay too. Paul stated in Romans 14:23b that "**everything that does not come from faith is sin.**"

This situation brings to mind the story of Jesus and Peter. In this story Jesus found a unique way to obtain money to satisfy a temple tax. In Matthew 17 it states:

> "After Jesus and his disciples arrived in Capernaum, the collectors of the two-drachma temple

tax came to Peter and asked, "Doesn't your teacher pay the temple tax?"

"Yes, he does," he replied.

When Peter came into the house, Jesus was the first to speak. "What do you think, Simon?" he asked. "From whom do the kings of the earth collect duty and taxes—from their own children or from others?"

"From others," Peter answered.

"Then the children are exempt," Jesus said to him. "But so that we may not cause offense, go to the lake and throw out your line. Take the first fish you catch; open its mouth and you will find a four-drachma coin. Take it and give it to them for my tax and yours," Matthew 17:24-27.

Can you imagine if Peter, upon finding the coin in the mouth of the fish, decided to laminate it for his scrapbook, put a hole in it to wear it as a necklace, or frame it and hang it on the wall? I can see the inscription beneath it now: "Here is the gold coin that Jesus made appear in a fish's mouth for payment of the temple tax." Think of how ridiculous that would have been. The entire purpose of the coin was to pay a debt, or at least a perceived debt, in this case. Let's face it, Jesus was rich. He had Judas as a treasurer because someone had to keep track of all the money that people gave him. I don't know a single person who is both flat broke and has a financial manager working for them.

The purpose of this miracle was two-fold. One, Jesus got the coin for the tax because he didn't actually owe the tax and therefore he had no intention of taking his money to pay it. Two, he wanted to teach Peter something about divine provision, even to the point of God taking care of wants, not just needs. If Peter had memorialized the coin, it would have been clear that he missed the point of the miracle entirely. Likewise, God is interested in not just our needs, but our wants as well. Whether we need to sell a gem to make money or not is unrelated to whether we may sell them. God really doesn't mind if we sell them, and if at any point He does, He will let us know.

Since the Bible seems pretty clear that we each have options on what we do based on our own faith level, and that God sometimes will gift us with supernatural resources to provide for specific needs, what about me personally—what have I done with them? In addition to the thousands of stones people have found in our house during Gem Parties, I personally have given away hundreds of them. We have a few necklaces with pendants made of gems, and I have a number of stones set aside for earrings for myself and my wife. I have never sold any gems, but it's not because I haven't tried—they are just hard to sell. Truth be told, making money off gemstones isn't as easy as one might imagine. Each stone has to be tested by a gemologist and certified for its value, and this costs money, especially without knowing in advance if the stone is even worth the cost of the appraisal.

Many of the gems that appear are semiprecious stones and typically aren't worth very much from a monetary perspective. Even the larger stones that might be worth more, especially the clear stones, are a risk. The reason is that just because it is a clear stone doesn't make it a diamond. It could easily be white sapphire, or a score of other stones almost no one has ever heard of: chrysoberyl, white spinel, achroite, enstatite, phenoite, and many others. In other words, just being a clear stone doesn't tell us anything other than that the stone is clear. Additionally, each stone has a varying level of clarity and as previously mentioned, some of the gems are flawed with visible cracks and chips. If someone doesn't already have a personal connection with a jeweler or ample free cash they are willing to risk, appraising them will be difficult. Once appraised, how does one go about selling the stone? Good question. That's also why it's not easy.

At the end of the day when regarding what to do with the stones, there really is no right or wrong answer. Whatever we each decide to do in regards to selling or not selling is between us and God and is not open to other peoples' judgments. It is a good idea to pay attention to whom we tell about selling the gems as some people will be far less receptive than others, but that is just wisdom and the same goes for the miracle as a whole. My encouragement is to firmly settle in our hearts first what we believe we are to do based on our beliefs and conversations with God and then step forward with giving them away, selling, or keeping them based on our decisions. In this process, remember one thing: God is a God of grace and love and if we misunderstand His will, He is very kind and forgiving and tends to give us more opportunities to get it right. If we feel we have done the wrong thing, we simply talk to God about it. He has already forgiven us for it and isn't holding it against us—we must not hold it against ourselves. The gems are, among other things, for personal enjoyment, and if we get so stressed about what to do with them that we no longer enjoy them as a gift from God, we are missing the point.

Chapter 5
Dealing with Feelings

We sat comfortably in the living room—I and probably a dozen or so other adults are chatting and getting acquainted. Small children were in and out laughing and totally accepted, at home among the adults. I thought to myself this could be any home in America, and I hoped to learn more of the extraordinary appearance of gemstones that I had heard about. I was not disappointed—a man got up and began walking to the kitchen, and almost immediately the children followed laughing and squealing "I got one!" and "Here's one!" and again "I saw one fall there!" Before my eyes they were collecting random gemstones of different sizes and colors where nothing had been before.

"What did I just see and how does he do it?" I asked a new friend who sat next to me. I asked if they fell out of his pockets. She laughed and said, "No, they just fall out of the air when he is around." She then said to wait and watch and maybe I would see some too. Not long after, the children found one next to me on the sofa, and again in front of me on the floor, then again and all along the pathway back into the kitchen. I really kept wondering how that man did that.

The man returned to his seat and talked with us but to be honest I cannot even remember what he said—my mind was busy wrestling with how he did that. Even as he sat and visited with us, occasionally I would hear a slight noise like a very small pebble dropping on the kitchen flooring behind us, and the children would immediately squeal and scramble and find another gemstone that had not been there before. I was truly puzzled. Obviously God was doing something delightfully unusual and surprising (to me) here but some of the others were used to it and showed mild amusement and seemingly joy at the appearance of these stones that seem to follow the presence of that man and his wife.

I felt strangely comfortable and at home with this group of people and enjoyed getting to know a few of them (I had met Michael King at another gathering a few months prior). I had to leave this gathering early because I lived quite a ways away, and upon learning that Michael and some others gathered around me and prayed for me. It was a prayer so right on about the current challenges in my life and that God would intercede for me and bless me. How did they know, because I hadn't told anyone some of this stuff?

Then some adults and all of the children who had found gemstones and were delighted to be gifted with them, they gave their gemstones to me—a clear baggie with way more than a dozen and one large purple one and a smaller clear yellow one and all sorts of pretty other colors, clear and sparkly in the light. Really??? This was a rare and precious and unusual gift and they were gifting me with the blessing that God had gifted them with. I was honored and touched and amazed and puzzled all at the same time. What is it within them, I thought, even the children, that they would happily give to me, a stranger to most, that which had just been a precious and wondrous gifting to them? Even more than the gems, I wished I had that kind of heart. I thought about this all the 50 some miles back home and for weeks after.

I related the happening to my family and their immediate response was disbelief and they didn't want to hear any more, but they could not deny the "happy" that seemed to surround me like a cloud for weeks after. And the gems? Well, that is such an interesting question, because I planned to take them to a jeweler and have them verified to see what they were. I expected them to be unusual either in type or cut because to me they were gems from heaven. But time marched on and although I thought of them often, I never made it to the jewelers but kept them in their original bag hidden under the jewelry in my tackle box. Yes that is where I keep my jewelry, lol.

As all life changes, suddenly so did mine and I needed to make an immediate move. I packed all my most valuable things in my car including the little tackle box where the gemstones lay hidden and began my process of moving, only to have the window of my car smashed out and everything in my car stolen two days later, including, yes, the gemstones that were so precious to me. I thought about it for days afterwards, even when there was no recovery of my things, and certainly not the little gemstones. They went to the street people who broke into my car. Seriously? Over time I have thought of that time and time again and I still do, and laugh. How fitting—how appropriate that those little gems would land in the hands of those who steal?

Jesus loved all people, still does. I think He had a sense of humor I can appreciate because He knows I already have the gift of the gems deep in my heart, the memory and experience that no one can take from me.

I'm good with that, but those who stole and got my gems in the process may not realize they have just been blessed and touched by God because I believe everything has energy and emits energy and they have taken into their lives an extraordinary extra-special manifestation of God's love that they don't even know about.

I cannot predict what will happen but nothing God does is wasted. I think above the gifting of the gems and new friendships that day at the King's house (lol how fitting is that), and how I also experienced the undeserved gift of Gods generosity through his children. Somehow I believe their gifting me and blessing me in such a manner grew in my heart the same spirit and I can say "God Bless those who hold the gems. God works behind the scenes— may His love and energy draw them to Him in amazing ways, as He has drawn us!" The story is not over, we just don't yet know the ending, and I am blessed!

J Linda Stevens

****

When I was wrapping up loose ends and getting this book ready to publish, I had a few encounters, including close to one hundred gems appearing in our house again over an afternoon, during which I realized I was leaving a very important topic out of this book. The next night I had a simple dream which illustrated the point and confirmed to me that this chapter needed to be written. The dream is as follows:

I was standing in the hallway of either a high school or college, and I saw another student walk by with a gallon-sized resealable plastic bag full of gems. And when I speak of gems, I'm not talking two millimeters in size. No, many of these gems were at least an inch or two long. One gem in particular, a sort of tan-yellow teardrop-shaped stone, was huge—almost the size of a coffee mug! I glanced at the bag and thought to myself "Why does he get them that size and not me?" In the dream, I also realized that this was becoming a more common phenomenon, such that random people were walking around in public carrying these gems and nothing strange was thought of it, except for me. I could sense a small amount of jealousy and disappointment in my own heart and recognized that while I didn't want that other student to not have gems, I would really like to have ones that size myself! With that, the dream ended.

The dream itself showed me three things. First, we are all still in a learning process. None of us have this all "figured out" at this point, and the truth is, we probably never will. Second, I have feelings surrounding this manifestation that I need to address—most specifically jealousy and disappointment. The third thing this dream did is act as a confirmation—if I am dealing with these things and they are showing up in my house, how much more may others go through this when they are only seeing it from afar?

The first time I saw gems fall my mind was blown away. The second and third times a little less so, until each time after that it my faith level for them being able to appear has increased. In spite of that fact, even to this day I struggle believing that they will appear, and that God wants them to manifest for me personally instead of me-as-one-of-a-group-of-people-present-when-they-appear. I have found gems so many times, both with others and by myself that it might be astounding to some to hear me share this, but I am being honest and fully transparent when I say so. Please understand my heart—I don't say this to belittle anyone else or make myself sound underprivileged when I realize that many would go great lengths just to have the experiences I have had to date. No, the reason I share this is because I believe others may have similar thoughts and feelings and need to hear direct, to-the-point honesty about emotional matters and the struggles I have gone through in this process as well as some tools on how to walk through them.

Let me just say that I think it is perfectly normal that we have difficulty when we see God bless others in some way but we do not have that same experience. It can often feel like God likes someone else more than us or that someone else has some "special connection" to God that we don't, even though, to my knowledge, the good news of Jesus is that there are no special connections anymore—God doesn't hold one person up as more valuable than another. We are all precious in His sight! Yet, some have the gems and others don't, so it is hard to see experientially how this can be true. Let's look at a few Bible passages and see what they say about this. Acts 10:34-35 says, "Then Peter began to speak: 'I now realize how true it is that God does not show favoritism but accepts from every nation the one who fears him and does what is right.'" God doesn't play favorites! If he did, then God would be guilty of discriminating and would be a judge with evil thoughts himself, which is impossible!

Matthew 5:45b says, "He causes his sun to rise on the evil and the good, and sends rain on the righteous and the unrighteous." In other words, if God isn't going to be picky about who He lets experience sunshine and rain, so why would He discriminate about other things? I know people who aren't followers of Jesus who have even had gems show up! I believe that in the times that some people have an experience and others look on wishing and hoping for those same experiences that there are a few mechanisms in play, which will help us to have these encounters ourselves. I will cover this in a later chapter titled "How Can I Have This Happen?" but now want to look at part of what God is doing when it looks like He is ignoring us to pick someone else.

The truth is that God doesn't pick some and ignore others like we might think, but rather has a plan and a purpose with a goal, and based on how He set up the laws of creation, requires our help for them to happen on earth. The main reason I understand that God causes gems to appear for some and not others is that God uses forerunners to release anything new into the earth realm. These forerunners are essentially the first seed-sowers of the glory, and as they take the heat from the demonic realms and the other people whom the demons use, they sow seeds of the glory God has endowed them with. As these seeds grow and bear fruit and more faith is released through these experiences, more people begin to experience the manifestation until it becomes common in the Body of Christ.

Salvation by Grace was brought back to the Body this way. The Baptism of the Holy Spirit and the operation of the Gifts of the Spirit were restored to the Body in similar fashion. The gold-dust miracle and the miracle of the gemstones have also happened in this manner. Truthfully, I do not even consider myself a forerunner in the true sense of the word, as this has been publicly happening in the Body of Christ for almost ten years at the time of writing this. Yet, in all honesty I am probably part of a second generation of those who are forerunning this spiritual sign that God is releasing in a greater measure in the earth. There is coming a day where this manifestation will grace homes all around the world to the point that it becomes normal for gems to manifest and abnormal if they do not, and God has planned for your home to be one of them!

Until that time, however, we each must learn to recognize and address the heart issues that arise as we pursue the experience of this blessed gift from heaven. Most heart issues spring from places of inner wounding and brokenness, as well as from incorrect beliefs we have about God and ourselves. To deal with these feelings we must understand where they come from, so we will take a look at doubt and unbelief, jealousy, and disappointment as the main heart problems that arise from this manifestation, and look at how to overcome them.

At the root of doubt and unbelief is an identity issue. When we come to a deeper understanding of who God created us to be, that God breathed from His spirit into molded earth and created us and that we are made in His image—essentially mini-gods designed to mirror His deity, we will come to understand just how much God loves and values us. How can He not? If we truly understood what it means that we are made in God's image we would not struggle with doubt over issues such whether God wants us to experience this gem miracle or not. We would understand that He has gifted us with creative power and wants us to use that ability to transform the earth, following the directions he gave to Adam in the beginning. When we are in doubt it is because we don't really understand our identities as children of God and that God is training us to rule and reign with Him! As we grow in understanding of what God is growing and maturing us into it will be impossible for unbelief to remain.

While doubt is an identity issue, at the root of the jealousy and disappointment is a love issue. When we feel unloved by God, jealousy and disappointment can have an open door to be planted in our hearts. As we deepen in the revelation that God truly and unconditionally loves us, even if we are struggling with these feelings, we will begin to be more settled within ourselves. While the issues may not be fully settled in our hearts, we will be able to give those feelings over to God and release them to Him, letting Him purify our emotions and only God can. As this occurs we will be able to do as the Bible says—to prefer one another over ourselves in our hearts, rejoicing with those who rejoice (Romans 12:10 and 12:15).

While it can be easy to say this, and it sounds nice on paper, it can be difficult to do these things in the actual moment. At one gem meeting we held there was a large purple gem that appeared which I found. This was the very first large gem that ever appeared in our house, and the only one to ever appear during the Gem Parties. It came with a silver setting already attached. I showed a few people and, not realizing what had happened, they gave it away to someone else. I didn't speak up at that moment, which hindsight showed me I should have, and that individual made an announcement to the entire room about how this gem meant something to them from God and how they were going to give it away to another ministry somewhere because of some loss that ministry had experienced. I will be honest, I agonized over that the rest of that night and had a very difficult time dealing with it. After a series of mishaps, over which I think everyone else involved was very gracious (and I can only hope I was too), I did receive the gem back and that ministry was still blessed with a number of other stones, but there was a real issue of anger that I was failing to deal with well in that moment.

If the soil of the heart is poorly tended, events like this one can allow seeds of jealousy and disappointment to plant themselves. Left untended, this jealousy and disappointment will grow to stunning heights and will certain bear fruit—but that fruit will only further poison the host and those around him or her. On top of that, demons will encourage the growth of these seeds. Demons, by their own choices, were cut off from the power supply from God in heaven. In order to become powerful they must steal our power, and as such they specialize in methods that tear us down, all the while sucking energy from our souls. One of the main ways they do this is by whispering lies into the ear to set each of us on a wrong path. As we continue down this path they are able to degrade our identities and steal more of our power. The problem is that we start by believing these thoughts that come into our head, and then we believe they are actually our own thoughts when they aren't. I have listed a few of the main lies the enemy will try to tell us in regards to this manifestation, as well as how these lies attack our own self-worth and faith.

God doesn't think you have earned it. This lie attacks the very root of the gospel of grace itself—namely that it is by grace we receive the many gifts from heaven, not by our own efforts. This type of lie not only sows serious doubt, but can cause one to go to great lengths to work to prove to God that one is deserving, thereby undoing the very grace that God extends to us all.

You're not pure enough to have this. This lie hits at the gospel as well, as though by our own efforts we can become holy or pure, which has never been the case, ever. It also feeds disappointment and enhances the working of the religious spirit in one's heart.

God will do it for them, but He won't do it for you. This lie feeds the doubt and jealousy, pitting us against others in our hearts, creating an "us versus them" mentality where one should never exist.

God only chooses a special few for this miracle-sign. This lie goes against everything that God stands for in the New Testament. James 2:1-4 says, "My brothers and sisters, believers in our glorious Lord Jesus Christ must not show favoritism. Suppose a man comes into your meeting wearing a gold ring and fine clothes, and a poor man in filthy old clothes also comes in. If you show special attention to the man wearing fine clothes and say, "Here's a good seat for you,' but say to the poor man, 'You stand there' or 'Sit on the floor by my feet,' have you not discriminated among yourselves and become judges with evil thoughts?

All of these lies can take hold when we begin to ponder them in our hearts. What if this is only something God does for a few special people and He doesn't want to do it for me? What if I am not pure enough and haven't earned this? Stop those thoughts!! Any time you begin to let your mind wander down that path, it will only lead to disappointment. Do not open your heart or mind to such considerations, as they are simply and only demonic lies meant to keep you from the gifts God has given you as your birthright. Yes, miracles such as gemstones are yours simply because you are God's child—no other reason is needed! As the son or daughter of the King of the Universe, everything He has is yours as well! It is important to guard your heart and your thoughts, taking every thought captive. If it doesn't agree with the truth then there is a good chance it wasn't your thought to begin with and was a demonic whisper attempting to plant seeds of corruption. If you don't consider those thoughts, the seeds die where they stand without ever planting, much less bearing negative fruit.

While we all need to be vigilant, I want to remind you that I am by no means perfect nor have I completely arrived here myself. At times I still struggle in a place of doubt and unbelief and fight jealousy and disappointment. There have been a number of occasions in this past year alone where I have found a single stone here or there where no one else may have been around, but more recently it seems that the gems appear around my stepdaughter and her family more than they do around my wife and me, even though we all live in the same house! In fact, when my stepdaughter lived elsewhere her family had gems showing up when we had none, and we were the ones who had hosted all of the gem parties in the first place! This is not simply a once-and-done thing for most people, where one encounter settles the issue in our hearts. We must continue to be vigilant against emotional issues and demonic lies that want to worm their way in and destroy the fruit of our hearts.

To help with this, I have learned what I refer to as a "one-minute prayer" that I find very useful when unwanted and negative emotions bubble up from within me that I feel unable to control or that I want to release. I provide a short template below, but it can be altered however fits the needs of the individual praying it. It works best if you pick one emotion at a time and pray through it until that emotion is no longer present or is no longer the emotion presenting itself, then move on to the next prominent emotion until there are no negative emotions left.

> "Heavenly Father, I don't want to feel _____ (the primary emotion) right now. I give You the feelings of _____ (primary emotion) and ask You to heal every wound and broken place that has caused it. In its place I ask that You give me _____ (insert opposite, positive emotion(s) here) and I receive this now by faith in Jesus' name. Amen."

I have used this prayer more times than I can count, and I find it highly effective. At times I may have to pray through the same emotion a few times, but it is especially useful when a memory comes up that angers or saddens me, or when I get set off by a current life event, which in this case is the negative feelings brought out by the gem miracle.

Please don't misunderstand me in the writing of this chapter. I truly love it when God sends us gems, and I find great pleasure in it, as well as do experience God's love in the midst of it. Yet, at times I feel a bit like the father in Mark 9:24 who cried out to Jesus, "I do believe, help me overcome my unbelief!" I recognize, sadly, that disappointment is a common thread throughout this experience, as even my social media posts show a lot of it from people who wish that they, too, could experience this, some of whom who lament why God doesn't see fit to do it to them. My purpose for sharing this is so that we can all reach a more healthy emotional state in regards to the gems, and not only that but to provide practical tools to arrive at that place, such as the prayer shared above.

Another method I use with situations such as those above is to address not the emotions, but the erroneous beliefs I hold surrounding a situation. To explain further, in any circumstance where I am hurt, angry, or upset by something God is doing, there is probably a conscious or subconscious belief I have that isn't accurate, and that inaccurate belief leads me to unrealistic expectations from God, causing me to get upset. We all have these beliefs, but not everyone knows what to do about them. For me, I start to force-feed myself a more accurate perspective.

I begin by asking myself questions: "Why do I feel this way? What are the wrong beliefs I have that are causing this?" After I identify the wrong beliefs I begin to "replace" them by bombarding myself verbally with beliefs and ideas that I think more accurately display the underlying truths in the situation. For me that usually looks like quoting Bible verses out loud to myself off the top of my head that speak to the issues at hand. I find it works well for me and helps me to align myself with

God's truths about a situation, but it's not the only way to do it, and that method may not work well if someone doesn't have a high level of scriptural recall. Still, even just verbalizing a more accurate belief system, whether from a Bible verse or not, should help clarify the mental processes and help set the mind on a forward track. This process may need to be repeated more than once because it is an act that is overwriting the previous subconscious beliefs, especially if the old beliefs are long-held and firmly planted. However, regardless of how many times it takes, this method will produce results.

In the end, I encourage you to not let doubt, jealousy, unbelief, disappointment, or any other feeling or belief to hinder you from pursuing the goodness that God has for you with this miraculous sign. I had heard of it and asked God to do it for me for almost eight years before I ever experienced it for myself. I am not saying that it will take that long for you (and I pray it does not) but know that even if you do not see immediate fruit that you can be in it for the long-haul and to stay the course in prayer, for God is a good God and gives gifts freely to those who ask Him.

Chapter 6

Tasting the Fruit

There is only so much that can be said through my words alone. I firmly believe that the testimonies of others speak loudly to what God is doing in and through this miracle. This is why testimonies are spread throughout the book, but I have compiled a collection of people's stories here which are by no means comprehensive. A great many more people are experiencing this than the few who have shared here. It is my hope that these will encourage you wherever you are in your own life, and that God pours his love and blessings out on people of all walks of life and who have a wide range of reactions to this miracle.

****

I'm not one to just believe things because you tell me that they're true. It's not that I don't trust people, it's that I don't like feeling as though someone has made a fool of me, so I watch things with what I hope is healthy skepticism no matter how much I want to believe that something is true.

When I arrived at the first "party," the room was abuzz with people talking about God's goodness and "Why would He do such a thing" and "What is His point." It all seemed to be centered on one guy, and when he got up to move around the room, everyone began to pay attention to his path because gems were going to show up where he had walked.

The host showed me some gems that had already shown up and I saw one and secretly wanted one like it. Within the hour one just like it showed up at my feet along with a couple of others. I was pretty sure that no one would have known my heart about it, so then I wanted to "see" them appear. I wanted to watch where none were and see them appear from nothing—and that's just how it was. The man walked by, the path was bare, I watched and saw nothing, then a shine and then the gems were there, before my eyes.

At one point the man and the host hugged and there was an explosion of gems that covered and area of about 7 feet square Everyone was looking at them and talking about God's goodness and how it is better to love one another.

Todd Adams

****

In early 2013, I was invited to Michael and Sunshine King's home in Portland, Oregon. A ministry couple who had traveled down from Washington State were going to be ministering. I had heard that wherever the husband went to minister, gems appeared supernaturally as he was ministering. Well . . . I just had to see this. I knew something supernatural was happening, but I just wanted to see it with my own eyes. My husband, who was a little more skeptical but willing to see, went along too.

We had an incredible time. There seemed to be an ebb and flow in the manifestation of the gems. We had a regular home group meeting—just going about our "business" of worshipping, eating, fellowshipping and visiting. The minister also shared his testimony and gave a short lesson. At various times throughout the time we were there, all of the sudden, gems would just appear on the carpet. Whoever saw them manifest would let out a cry, and everyone would excitedly dive for one! It was so thrilling! One second they were not there, and then suddenly, there they were! Right before our eyes! It was shocking!

At first, as we do, the natural mind tries to figure out a non-supernatural explanation. My husband was thinking well now, wait a minute. Maybe the man is just somehow shaking them out of his pant-leg as he walks along. My husband was sitting in an office chair next to a computer desk, observing the meeting. As he was thinking these things, a gem appeared right by his foot. He knew no one had been walking there. That's when he was like ok, something supernatural is happening here! That was our first exposure to the gems. We both went home excitedly with a pouch of jewels we had collected throughout the three or four hours we had been there.

I have to interject right here, that it does change you. We know things sometimes manifest from another realm into this realm. We know that people who have received new body parts from another realm and deposited into this realm. But it was internal, so we didn't get to actually witness it with our eyes. We had had lost items reappear in strange places, and suspected angels had brought them to us and placed them there. But we didn't actually see it happen, right before our eyes. The appearing of the gems, however, was a direct manifestation from the other realm of a concrete item that we got to WITNESS happen. We just felt so honored that the Kings had invited us and that we got to witness it! How many Christians would love to witness this!?! It was such an honor to be there. And like I said—it does change you. Once you have seen things manifest from another realm, you are much more open for it to happen in any area of your life. We tend to believe our past experience. And now, once you have seen it, your past experience is that it DOES happen! Once you've seen it, you can't go back. Who would want to?

At the time, my husband and I were not yet married. He kept his collection of heavenly gems at his bedside. In his collection of gems, he had received two that looked like traditional cut diamonds—one clear and one a very pale yellow. The yellow one was much larger than the clear one, about twice as large. About a week or two after the gem party, we were astonished to notice that the clear one had grown and was now much larger than the yellow one.

I read that heavenly gems will sometimes change if you have them near to you, to try and reflect what is in your spirit. After I read that, I started keeping mine beside my bedside as well, and also wore some in a necklace locket so they would be close to me. I have noticed various changes in size and shape of several of them. They are excellent conversation-starters as well.

I gave my friend Lila a necklace locket with heavenly gems. She wears them constantly and has witnessed to countless people using the gems. She says people stare at them, are drawn in, and can't seem to take their eyes off of them.

In August of 2013, I was privileged to hold a Gem meeting in my home in Albany, Oregon. Over 60 people were in attendance throughout the day, and all went home with gems. When I scheduled the meeting, my thinking was still that they will manifest only in that minister's presence. I believed it to be his unique anointing, and that was it. To blow up my paradigm, God had two gems appear, one in my bathroom and one on my dining room floor as we were cleaning house, getting ready for the meeting. After the meeting was over, at 11 p.m. at night, we found some outside at the curb where the man's car had been parked. My husband and I carefully went over the entire house after all the guests had gone home, even moving the living room furniture, making sure we hadn't missed a thing. But the next day there were more gems. On the kitchen counter, nestled in the living room carpet, or wherever. And the day after that. And after that. This went on pretty much daily for several weeks after the party. And to a little lesser degree for several more weeks after that. So much for thinking it only happened in that minister's presence. He had left Oregon and gone home to Washington the day after the meeting. Unless he was really good, I don't think he can shake anything out of his pant-leg from there.

I have probably been to a total of six home meetings now where the gems are manifesting. You never get tired of the miracle. It is always a thrill to see things manifest. I still occasionally receive a gem from the Lord that appears in my home, just for me. When I do, it is so very personal, each and every time.

Rebecca VanSpeybrock

****

A minister was ministering at Turning Point Church in Nicholasville, Kentucky this last weekend. My husband Paul and I had been invited by a friend to come and be with him for these meetings. We had no prior meeting or knowledge of that minister or his wife.

Our friend Logan kept emailing us about "this guy" who had water turn into wine in his house (He never mentioned the manna, gold dust, or gemstones that were also appearing in this man's meetings). We took a four-hour journey from Nashville and headed northeast to Eastern Kentucky, right smack in the middle of horse country. We arrived at another friend's house in the late afternoon.

The first thing I noticed about the minister is that he was covered in gold dust. Yeah, I know that's been happening all the time in meetings, nothing new, right? This wasn't a meeting; this was a casual lunch. No one had been speaking, praying, or even worshipping! What had been going on was Holy laughter, people getting drunk from communion using manna and the "new" wine and just basic fellowship with others. Holy laughter, drunken singing, glory dust all over the place, even in the brownies? Wow, we walked into a glory bomb! So, I figured we might as well join them! Things got really fun then.

His wife pulled out a wooden box and started showing everyone some of the gems that had fallen recently. Actually two identical diamonds had appeared in the box upon their arrival at that house (at least that is when they think they appeared because they hadn't opened the box since leaving their house in SC). They had never had two come at once before. There were about six or seven gems in the box total. People were about as slain in the spirit or drunk as you can get and still function. Once the meeting started, he began sharing how God began doing supernatural things in his house (this was at the church). The first thing to happen to them was that manna began to appear on their mantle. Sometimes it would be on the pages of the open bible, other times there would be piles of manna in the shape of a circle.

When we first got to the meeting, the minister sat down on the front pew and I was standing behind him. I looked down at his hair and there was a pile of gold dust there, off to the side a little bit that was at least 1-inch tall (the "pile" had not been there at the other house). During the night it moved to different places on his head. His face, neck, and shoulders were also covered in gold dust.

When he began sharing on the importance of having communion every day, the first diamond fell (Exodus 24:9, Zechariah 9:14, John 6:43). As you can imagine, it created quite a stir! It was like a portal opened up about knee high and this diamond tumbled out. It happened really fast; one minute there was nothing on the carpet and the next, there it was (I did not get to take a picture of this one). There were other things that the lord blessed us with that night. The meeting ended with everyone taking communion with the manna and the new wine. I don't know if it was by faith or if it was by angelic assistance or a little of both, but I sure felt a physical difference in my body (also in my spirit) afterwards.

The following afternoon worship involved a lot of angelic activity . . . can't explain anything more than that. Some saw them with their spiritual eyes and some with one of the five senses. I heard rain falling and wings all around me, but only had impressions visually. It was during this worship session as the pastor of the church came over to the minister on his knees and said, "I want this! I want to see these things, I want my church to move in this!" that the next diamond fell! In my spirit I heard "2 carats." Wow! He spoke on seeing those angels we co-labor with, and a fire tunnel was formed by those who already see angels so that those who do not would have an impartation of that gift and faith. My husband Paul saw many angels coming in the room to participate in the impartation. It was a very powerful time . . . lots of "train wrecks" so to speak, and also lots of impartation and people beginning to see the angels they were co-laboring with! This meeting concluded with communion also.

The last session was Saturday evening. After worship, the minister spoke on Keeping the Joy and Putting on the Holy Spirit (see Romans 14:17). While he was showing how to put on the Holy Spirit (picture putting on a wetsuit, stepping in, etc.), another diamond fell on the floor at his feet. After this, he wanted to pray over the worship leader and his wife. While this ministry was taking place, the fourth and final diamond fell. The next day at this church, a blind eye was opened and arthritis was completely healed. Prophetically you could say this church can now SEE and is free to MOVE in the things of God!

Ginny Wilcox

****

When Michael King called and asked if I wanted to come to his house for a Gem Party, the first thought that ran through my head was, "What is a Gym Party?" I honestly had no idea. "Was it where we got together and lifted weights? What a weird thing to ask!" He soon clarified and I found myself perplexed once more. "Okay, now what is a Gem Party?" Following was a vague line explaining how it would be a great experience and a way to put off the inevitable Sunday night homework cram. And with that, he had me!

The following day and with not much to go on, I drove over to his house, all the while trying to make sense of this ambiguous Gem Party I had committed myself to attending. The ride was quick, but I could not suppress my intrigue, "Would there be actual gems?" I had hoped so, but my logical conscious mind suggested otherwise.

Michael and his wife Sunshine had been friends of my parents and I had met them on a few social occasions, but other than that our relationship was hardly established. Upon pulling up to his house, I quickly learned it was a party indeed for cars filled the driveway and had begun piling along the street, almost to the point of blocking traffic. My excitement amplified and after passing through the front door an electrifying energy shook my body. There was no music. There was no alcohol. This was not the normal college party I was used to, but the energy was unmatched by anything I had ever witnessed.

My eyes shifted, scanning the room in an attempt to gather even the slightest parcel of information, something that would help me decode the meaning for this gathering. Amidst smiles and roaring laughter, I managed to catch a glimpse of a small gem, but before I could go investigate, Michael came out and drew my attention away. We then began catching up, from how's school and work, to what was new with him, but the real questions I had were about these gems, so I asked him. Cheerfully and full of energy, he began to explain to me something I had a hard time believing, but I will never forget, "We are gathered here to worship the Lord and witness the manifestation of the spiritual realm through Heavenly gems."

Michael continued telling me of his experience regarding these gems and how they worked, explaining that through prayer, gathering, and speaking in prophetic tongues, they would simply appear. At this point, I grew skeptical, even after having caught a glimpse of a gem just moments before. Perhaps it was an indicator of how irrational this all seemed. Perhaps I had a hard time believing in something that I had yet to experience, and even more so, it didn't make sense logically.

Nevertheless, he encouraged me to grab some food, sit down, and keep an eye out for gems. He explained that they all took different shapes and sizes and often ended up on the carpet, so I followed his instructions and kept a stern watch on the floor, something I assume looked quite silly.

His house was fairly packed at this time, with easily a dozen people, so I quickly started up a conversation and before we could even surpass the greeting, someone else yelled out from over the noise, "I've got one!" Immediately I looked over, mind racing at how this could be. She then stood from the floor holding a small gem in her palm. It was green and perfectly cut, no larger than a pebble. In an attempt to keep my sanity, I began trying to rationalize the occurrence. My eyes could see the gem, I could feel it with my hands, but I was no gemologist. What if this jewel was a fake? What if she simply pulled it out of her pockets to create a ruse, allowing me to fall into a line of disbelief?

A good half hour passed like this, every five or so minutes someone calling out over the crowd with a glistening jewel in their hand, enthralled and ever cheerful. From this point, I decided I must get myself one of these gems. "If they were real, I might be able to make some serious money. After all, diamonds are quite a treasured commodity," I thought. With this mentality I sat for a good 20 minutes, scouring the room, hoping to find my very own diamond, and all the while people continued gathering their own.

Jealousy swept over me like a plague and I began to feel left out and separated – disconnected from those who had their very own gems. Now I wanted one for two reasons. First, to make some money and second, to feel like a part of the group. I quickly became frustrated and thought about leaving when Michael came and sat next to me. Without saying a word he handed me a small baggy with three small gems inside and I sat in confusion. "You are just giving these to me?" I asked, "Are they not treasured and valuable?" At that moment, I was overwhelmed by his grace and felt belonging, even though I had yet to find my own gem.

"We have plenty here and they are valuable, but I want you to have these," he said with an ear-to-ear grin. My perspective now was completely changed and instead of seeking the jewels for my own reward and my own gain, I sought them out for another reason entirely. I wanted to witness God's power!

A few more minutes passed and people began to leave, but I had still yet to find a gem. I was sitting in my own area and no one had passed by for a few minutes. I began praying, thanking the Lord for this experience and many other things, for it had been some time since I had prayed last. I opened my eyes half-hoping to see a gem sitting in front of me and when I did, there was nothing. I will admit, I was slightly disappointed, but I glanced away for a millisecond and when I looked back, there was a small gem in from of me, resting so elegantly on the carpet. Intrigued and overwhelmed, I quickly snatched it up and began to investigate. It was simply stunning. I then began to doubt its legitimacy, but realized I was the only one in that area and no one had passed by, leading me to believe the gem was indeed from Heaven. "But how?" I did not know and I did not care to know, I simply believed.

How all of this happened, I can only rationalize as one of God's works. Was it a ruse and are the gems fakes? I do not know and I cannot say for certain, but I can confirm the legitimacy of them appearing out of thin air, and that in itself, is a miracle.

Daniel Hayes

****

People ask me, "Why the gemstones?" I believe it is just another way that God wants to manifest His love for us.

I am sure that our Father, who is an awesome, all-powerful sovereign God, is also a very good Daddy to His children. He is a Father who likes to give only good gifts to His children, to surprise them, play with them, and love on them. The gems, supernaturally appearing, is just one of them. I know this might sound simplistic to some, but His presence, love, joy, and excitement is what I have experienced.

I have had many opportunities to share about the gems and give them away when the Holy Spirit has directed me to. I then experience an increase of more gems. The people I have given them to have had different experiences, feelings, and emotions. Some have cried while they held them, feeling God's love. Some have been overwhelmed and overjoyed. Some have accepted God as real and present and have received Jesus as their Lord and Savior. Some are just curious and want to know more about Jesus, angels, and the heavenly realm. It's all been good and a wonderful opportunity to share God's love for them.

Our Father God is love and the supernatural manifestation of the gems is just one way that He is communicating His love for us and to us.

Judy Hope

****

Chapter 7

How Do I Have This Happen?

I was invited by Rebecca VanSpeybrock to her house for a Gem Party. I was intrigued and excited, I had put in a hard day working in the ER beforehand. When I walked into her house, the sweet presence of the Lord was so strong that I just soaked it up like a dry sponge. And then when we started worshipping, I was enthralled with even more of the love of our God. I could hear the clinking of Gems falling on the hardwood floor but did not want to take my focus off of Jesus. It felt wrong for me to take my eyes from Him to look for the gems and so I just kept my eyes on Him. When I was going to leave, Michael King asked if I had found any gems and when I said no, he gave me the ones he had found. I tried to refuse but he said he had more.

I was invited to another gem meeting the next day in Salem. While I was driving up there, the Lord told me to go have fun and look for gems like an excited child. He told me I would find a diamond, a pearl and an opal just for me! It was an amazing time of prayer, worship and seeing gems appear right before our eyes! The pearl that I actually found was a new dear friend, who God said was my pearl, Katherine Lyness-Smith and I found several different colors of gems. Included was a couple that look like diamonds, and another orange one with red streaks in it. But I did not find an opal and was confused until I found out later that the Orange stones are called fire opals! Yeah God!

This summer I had the privilege of hosting a meeting at my house. Many gems appeared and blessed those who came. It was thrilling! One of the stones that appeared at my feet was another fire opal but it was very special because it had a red circle around the perimeter and then a dark streak going to the center of it. I have always prayed for "bulls-eye prayers," my term for prayers that hit the mark. This gem looked like it had an arrow going to the center and hitting the Bulls-eye! Everywhere I go, I have my gems in my purse and share about them and let people pick out ones to keep. When we were in Pennsylvania this summer, I was sharing about this special gem and it was with the hand full of others, but when I went to put them away, it was gone. I searched all over the room, counter and emptied my purse over and over again. It was lost and gone. Here, back in Oregon, two months later it just appeared in my purse again!

I continue to give away the gems and yet have more appear and multiply. Also, I asked one girl what her favorite color was, and she said red, so I gave her one that was about 4 cm and looked like a ruby. I also gave her a tiny green one and as we were looking at them in her hand, the green one tripled in size! My son Gregory was with me and we all saw it get bigger! After the minister couple left, gems have continued to appear in my house, purse and even in my pants pocket at work. I love sharing about them and giving them away! It is so meaningful to see the joy and increased faith that they bring! I have watched my friends pursue God *even more and believe for things that did not seem possible after this. It has done the same for me, increased my hunger and faith for God and also makes me feel loved and special!*

My friend had great doubts about how real they were until I let her see and hold mine. I also let her pick out four of them and bought a locket for her to put them in. She had another gem appear in the locket and then a beautiful crystal appear on the carpet of her massage room! She was deeply touched! It is so fun going on treasure hunts and finding more gems and then being able to give them to others to enjoy and be blessed by! God is amazing, holy and yet He has such a fun side that loves to bring joy and laughter to us!

Cheryl Landis

****

The most frequent question I have been asked about gems is, "How do I get them to show up for me too?" This is a difficult question because it doesn't have a simple answer. In fact, this isn't something that is under my control so I can't "make them" appear for anyone, much less even myself. However, not having a "guaranteed method" to make them appear doesn't mean that I have learned nothing on my journey on how this happens and to encourage it to happen more. I believe a person can do a number of things to increase the likelihood of experiencing this manifestation, which I will explain.

Angels seem to play a significant role in this manifestation. When my wife and I first encountered the gems, it was very clear that angels were active in making gems appear or show up. In fact, at times people would see an angel at work spreading gemstones, and some other friends have claimed to see the same. Interestingly enough, Prophet Kat Kerr has spoken on this subject, stating in a YouTube message that she has seen angels scooping up handfuls of gems and throwing them through portals down to the earth. While I have not specifically seen angels doing any of these things, I have had a number of times where I could perceive where gemstones were about to appear next, and usually they would appear there a short time later. The significance of that to me is that I believe I was perceiving some sort of spiritual energy at work, and it makes sense to me that it could easily have been an angel that I was sensing. Additionally, I have seen in the spirit realm a great desert that is made up entirely of gemstones, even down to the tiny grains of sand—all precious stones!

The first time I saw this, I shared it with a friend who confirmed that he had seen the Gemstone Desert too! Gems are plentiful in heaven, so much so that the walls of the Heavenly City spoken of in Revelation 21 are made from them where it states,

> "The angel measured the wall using human measurement, and it was 144 cubits thick. The wall was made of jasper, and the city of pure gold, as pure as glass. The foundations of the city walls were decorated

with every kind of precious stone. The first foundation was jasper, the second sapphire, the third agate, the fourth emerald, the fifth onyx, the sixth ruby, the seventh chrysolite, the eighth beryl, the ninth topaz, the tenth turquoise, the eleventh jacinth, and the twelfth amethyst. The twelve gates were twelve pearls, each gate made of a single pearl. The great street of the city was of gold, as pure as transparent glass" (Revelation 21:17-21).

God sends his angels out from time to time to bring the literal fabric of heaven to us on the earth. Even as Jesus himself prayed, "Let your kingdom come, your will be done, on earth as it is in heaven" (Luke 11:2).

To see this in your own life, ask God to assign Gem-angels to you. It truly can be as simple as Matthew 7:7-8 says, "Ask and it shall be given to you; seek and you shall find; knock and the door shall be opened. For everyone who asks, receives; he who seeks, finds; and to him to knocks, the door shall be opened." It is God's pleasure to give you every good thing in His Kingdom, so don't be afraid to ask for what you want. If you don't receive it immediately, keep on asking over time until you do. God promises that if we ask, we WILL receive. In my case, it took asking over the course of years, but eventually, God not only fulfilled this promise in Scripture, but has told me there is more to come! He truly is faithful! Angels are also attracted to worship, so regular worship, while not in any way forcing the manifestation, will certainly increase the angelic presence in your home or gathering, and that can only help!

In addition to the activity of angels, I believe there is a gift of miracles associated with the gemstones. Why do they appear around some people in great force and around others minimally or not at all? A gift makes the most logical sense. When one operates in a gift, there is more of a direct pipeline from heaven in regards to that particular miracle. Thus, what might be extremely infrequent for one person who doesn't have a gift will be a regular occurrence for someone who operates in that particular grace. Not only that, but different individuals will have that gift operating at different levels and strengths, so the frequency and peculiarity of the manifestation will vary greatly. Knowing that there is a spiritual gift associated with the gems, I asked the man who ministered the gems to lay hands on me and pray for me on multiple occasions to receive this grace as well. I firmly believe that if someone lays hands on me and prays for me to receive something spiritual that they operate in, I will receive it, although usually in what I refer to as "seed form."

When you receive a seed, it has the potential to grow into a spectacular plant, but until that seed is planted and watered, you can hold that it as long as you want and nothing will happen. Likewise, spiritual gifts operate much like seeds. When someone lays hands on you and prays for you to receive the gift, it is the same as them handing you a seed. What you *do* with that seed over time is what will make all the difference in the world. Mentally putting that seed on a shelf and not continuing to pray that it grow and develop will yield no results. However, if that seed is tended through prayer and activating faith, and the weeds of doubt are rooted out from time to time, that seed has a better chance to flourish and bear much fruit.

Along with having someone pray and impart this spiritual gift to you, of equal benefit is simply getting around someone who operates in this manifestation. For whatever reason, many things are caught as much as they are taught. In other words, there is something about being around someone with a gemstone manifestation, or any other manifestation for that matter, that being in their presence tends to accelerate the growth in your own life. It is almost like there is some sort of spiritual resonance that takes place and entrains you into that manifestation the more you spend time around that person. I can't really explain it better than that, but just know that being around others with a gift may cause you to walk in it.

Possibly related to the rubbing-off on someone is the concept of a spiritual atmosphere. There are times that, when in the presence of another person, certain spiritual experiences happen more easily. Some examples for me are where prophecy or spontaneous worship flow more smoothly when around a highly prophetic friend. Mind you, I can normally prophesy or worship in spontaneous song anyway, but there are definitely times when it becomes many times smoother to flow in that ability, and I can always tell when it happens.

While I do believe angels are involved in the formation of these *easy* atmospheres, the other people we are around play a large part in that as well. My friend Beth, one of the God-junkies, has said before that she always gets more revelation when she is around our friend Hope. Just being in Hope's presence brings her increased revelation because Hope is a prophet and there is something about the Holy Spirit working in and through Hope that further enhances Beth's strong prophetic gifts.

The next step is to ask God to reveal new revelation to you. What is He saying and doing? Ask Him! Let the things He shares with you build your faith to see it happen! There was one point a few years ago, just after we first experienced this, where I began to pray and earnestly seek God. He told me to not pray for it and that He would take care of it. In all honestly, I was a bit disappointed at first, but I recognized that God told me not to pray about it because He wanted me focused on other things at that time. I also recognized that God was telling me not to pray about it because He already had the need taken care of—it wasn't something that needed deep, lengthy intercession, but rather was something He was already addressing and it involved timing that was completely different than what I was hoping for at first. Nevertheless, God is always right, so always do what you see your father doing! A year or so after God told me not to pray about having gems appear for me, we had our first Gem Party. A year or so after that, the gems began to earnestly appear for us! God's answer is yes, but there may be a timing issue. Ask

God for His timetable, as it may save you much in the way of frustration and heartache. God's answer might not be "no," but rather "wait just a little bit longer until it's time."

Don't get me wrong, God's timetable might be exceedingly frustrating to us. I am not exactly the most patient person, especially spiritually. I believe that Jesus already died for everything, so I should have *everything*, and right now, if not yesterday. When I pray for the sick or injured I expect them to get healed immediately, and honestly don't get why it doesn't always happen on the spot. My expectation is that God's goodness is for here and now always! In spite of that, God doesn't always see fit to do things on my timetable, and sometimes there are other factors in play I am unaware of. Just because something isn't happening now doesn't mean it won't happen sooner or later. A gentleman I bought a trailer from a few months back said to me, "God is rarely early, but he is always on time." Don't fret if things aren't happening in your timeframe. Get with God and listen for His timetable, and go from there.

On the other hand, having encouraged you to be patient and wait for God's timing, it is important to remember that not everything is about God's timing. Sometimes it is about praying through the warfare. After all, the enemy doesn't want us to be blessed, feel loved by God, or receive the good gifts He has for us. If the gems aren't appearing it may simply be that there is warfare you need to wade through for it to happen. Daniel Chapter 10 tells the story of Daniel's encounter with a heavenly being who had to fight against the Prince of Persia in order to successfully make it to Daniel to give him the message from heaven.

John Mulinde, an apostle in Africa, writes of a conversation he had with a former warlock in his essay "Combat in The Heavenly Realms: How Satan Stops our Prayers." Mulinde outlines what heavenly combat looks like, and how what we cannot see influences God's work in our lives. He relates:

> "Some prayers appear like smoke that drifts along and vanishes in the air. These prayers come from people who have sin in their lives that they are not willing to deal with. Their prayers are very weak; they are blown away and disappear in the air. Another type of prayer is also like smoke. It rises upward until it reaches the rock; it cannot break through the rock. These prayers usually come from people who try to purify themselves, but who lack faith as they pray. They usually ignore the other important aspects that are needed when someone prays. The third type of prayer is like smoke that is filled with fire. As it rises upward, it is so hot that when it reaches the rock, the rock begins to melt like wax. It pierces the rock and goes through (Mulinde)."

Mulinde continues that as people begin to pray, their prayers look like the first type. But as they continue praying, their prayers change and become like the second type of prayer. And as they continue praying, suddenly their prayers ignite into flames. Their prayers become so powerful that they pierce through the rock.

"Many times evil agents would notice that prayers were changing and coming very close to becoming fire. These agents would then communicate with other spirits on earth and tell them, 'Distract that person from prayer. Stop them from praying. Pull them out.' Many times Christians yield to these distractions. They are pressing through, repenting and allowing the Word to check their spirit. Their faith is growing. Their prayers are becoming more focused. Then the devil notices that their prayers are gaining strength, and the distractions begin. Telephones ring. Sometimes, in the middle of very, very intense prayer, the telephone rings and you think you can go answer it and then come back and continue praying. However, when you return, you go back to the beginning. And that's what the devil wants. Other kinds of distractions come your way. They may touch your body, bringing pain somewhere. They may make you hungry, causing you to want to go to the kitchen to prepare something to eat. As long as they can get you out of that place, they have defeated you. He said to the pastors, 'Teach the people to set aside some time, not just for some casual praying, they can do that the rest of the day. Once a day, they should have a time when they focus wholeheartedly on God, without any distractions.'"

"If the people persist in this kind of prayer and allow themselves to be inspired in the spirit and to keep going, something happens in the spirit. The fire touches that rock, and it melts. The man said that when the melting begins, it is so hot that no demon spirit can stand it. No human spirit can stand it. They all flee. They all run away. There comes an opening in the spiritual realm (Mulinde)."

The key from this passage above is that our prayers do make a difference and transform the heavens over us. When all is said and done, don't be afraid to fight it through!

In a recent conversation with Praying Medic we discussed an illustration that I believe shows a picture of what is going on when one person experiences a manifestation that others do not—an illustration that can help you to experience this yourself! Imagine a group of children all gathered around a gumball machine, and all of them are drooling over the multicolored gumballs before them. One girl steps forward, pulls a quarter out of her pocket, pops it in the machine, and turns the knob. Like clockwork, the levers turn and a gumball drops into the slot below, which the child promptly puts in her mouth and the corners of her lips turn up into a smile. Some of the other children look at her with disappointment, wishing they, too could have a gumball. One boy turns and runs away, only to return a minute later with a quarter as well and he, too, is rewarded with a gumball. Soon, some of the children scatter, returning with quarters as well, while some other children continue to stare disappointedly at the heartless machine that refuses to give them candy. A bit later someone else walks up with a stack of quarters and starts popping gumballs from the machine and handing them out left and right until a number of children who didn't have quarters of their own also get some candy.

Miracles, for all their unpredictability, do have a few predictable components. Much like putting a quarter in a machine, if you have the right currency, you can access miracles at any time. In this illustration then, God is like the gumball machine. He isn't partial about who gets to receive miracles or healing or anything else, but if the proper currency isn't present, it simply isn't going to happen. The first child used faith, the currency of heaven, to access the treasure. The second child, and those thereafter, didn't have the necessary faith, but they went out and got some and returned with fruit for their labors. The final child was someone who carried enough currency that it didn't matter if another child had any or not—theirs was sufficient for a number of people to access the treasure. In dealing with disappointment, it is partially not completely, a faith problem. If we, too, had faith, we would see more gems than we do now. While this can sound insulting to some, it's not meant that way at all. Rather, if low faith really is a problem, then much like a medical diagnosis, it can be hard to treat a problem until you know what it is. If low faith is your problem, then you can now do something about it! Don't be like the children who stare at the machine *hoping* they can have one, but look at how you can go out and get the faith you need for the manifestation.

It can be easy when hearing someone talk about faith to turn off your listening ears and glaze over. This happens to me sometimes, but I believe that it is partly because there is so little practical teaching on faith. Faith is a spiritual substance that is creative in nature. In other words, faith is the spiritual building block to all of reality, and it is the creative power of faith that God used when He spoke the heavens and the earth into existence. If faith can create the universe, then we, too, when using faith, can see miracles happen! If faith is an area of weakness for you, I encourage you to find ways to increase your faith and see what God opens up before you!

As I mentioned earlier, ask God and earnestly seek this manifestation. Don't be obsessive and striving to obtain it by works, but open yourself up in your heart and ask God honestly, and keep on asking over time. In my mind, this asking-and-seeking could go a few different ways. First, try to get around someone with the manifestation if possible as an act of earnestly seeking. Second, pray and keep on praying. You can't annoy God with your prayers. Third, see how you can alter your focus and build your faith. You might want to write yourself reminders or buy plastic gems (or even low-cost real ones at a rock shop) that you decorate a frequented area with to remind you that God is a gem-giver. My own trick of focus is that I have gotten used to picking up sparkly things. When I am walking down the street, in a store, or even around

94

the house, sometimes I will see something sparkle on the floor. When I see it, I stop and pick it up, whatever *it* might be.

True story, once, a few years ago I was at a conference and during worship I looked down and saw something sparkle on the floor. It was so small that I figured it was glitter, but I bent down and picked it up anyway. It was the *tiniest* gem I have ever seen in my life!! I feel like it would have been too small for human hands to cut, and I had to focus very closely to even be able to make it out. In fact, it was so small that even after putting it in a plastic baggie, I lost it some months later because the bag looked entirely empty, and I either accidentally gave it away or it fell out unnoticed! So keep looking because you never know when that something that sparkles will turn out to be the gem you didn't know you were asking for. Not only that, but when I go to pick up the sparkling object, regardless of what it is, I am building a habit of expectation that God will bless me with gems.

Sometimes I will find plastic gems on the ground outside in public, but I always thank God for them as they are a reminder of the other gems I have seen and the ones I expect to see in the future. I used to get frustrated at first that they weren't "real" gems, but at the same time they were reminders to me of God's glory and goodness and that one day I would see "real" gems appear. I used to have a container where I kept all these plastic gems I would find, which was my way of "sowing" into the gem manifestation. I wasn't sure how else to do it, so I would just treasure the plastic gems as gifts from

God and reminders of what I was asking Him for—letting them act as reminders of God's majesty and power, and also as a sort of thank-you to Him for His gifts to me. I encourage you to find your own creative reminders and ways to stretch your own faith and gratitude in this area, as a properly positioned heart can make all the difference in the world. If heart conditions are something you are struggling with, I encourage you to re-read the chapter on "Dealing with Feelings" and really pray through your heart-issues until you reach a place of resolution. Get help from someone else if necessary! Inner healing and deliverance are key components to being able to live as believers, and if this is shining light on places of darkness in your own heart, take the opportunity to be transformed by that light and get free in that area.

I know that many of you desire to have this manifestation in your own life, and that is what prompted you to read this book. Some of you are curious and want to know more but have never heard of this before. Regardless of your understanding or exposure level prior to now, I want you to experience this amazing and belief-changing miracle and I believe with all my heart that God wants everyone to have this experience. It is exciting to see God manifest his grace and love to us in such an overt, noticeable, tangible way, and what's more, it can be used as a tool to share the message of God's love with others. As we close, I'd like to pray for you to receive this manifestation that God has given my family and many others by his great grace:

Father, I ask that You grace each person who reads this today with the manifestation of gemstones from heaven, with supernatural oil, gold dust, feathers, and everything else You have for him or her. I ask that You give us all new opportunities to learn and grow in this reality, and to understand more and more about who You are in us. I ask that you adorn us as your bride and give us a dowry to give to our bridegroom, Jesus, that in our hearts we may be with Him where He is, even as He prepares a place for us. We thank You for Your goodness and grace, and we receive this gift freely because of Your great love for us in Jesus' name. Amen.

Bonus Chapter:

Coeur D'Alene and Puerto Rico

When I first published the Kindle version of *Gemstones From Heaven* in August of 2015, I had a few more stories I wanted to share but wasn't able to fit them into the book for a variety of reasons. Recently I found some old recordings via the internet, and after some transcribing and conducting more interviews, I pulled together the following stories. Even as I typed them up, I found myself getting excited yet again about this manifestation. I have shared my own experiences with the gemstones with many, and there is something about reading and hearing about the miraculous that keeps things fresh and new. Maybe it's the expectancy that rises in our hearts that this could happen to us too. Maybe it stirs up faith in the goodness of our extravagant God. Whatever it is, my hope in sharing these stories is to honor those who have both experienced the glories of this manifestation and also trudged through the difficult times when many turned against them for what God had done in their lives. I will forever be grateful for those who have walked this path ahead of me, and I hope these stories encourage and impact your life as they have mine.

Gemstones Fall in Coeur D' Alene

Gateway Christian Fellowship in Coeur D'Alene, Idaho had been praying for years to see God's glory manifest. In the early 2000s they had a Glory Explosion conference with Jeff Jansen, Joshua Mills, and David Herzog where gold crowns appeared in people's mouths, gold dust appeared on people's clothing and skin, and people lost weight instantly. Some had open visions and many people were healed. The church began to pray for the gemstone manifestation and for God's glory to appear. On June 8th of 2006, their prayers were answered. Early that day, one of the church leaders had a conversation with a couple who had experienced manifestations of gemstones and manna in their meetings. Within an hour of talking to that ministry couple, the church received a phone call from one of their parishioners, whose story is as follows:

One of Gateway Church's parishioners was a normal, hardworking man who God chose to touch in an unusual way. Terry arrived home from work and got out of his truck as he did every day. His wife Geri had come out of the house to help him bring his things in when she saw it fall. Terry turned toward it and when he saw the stone laying there, he bent down and picked it up— a stunning purple jewel. His wife asked if he had thrown it, but he pointed out they didn't have the kind of money one needed to casually throw gems on the ground. Excited, she ran into the house and called the church and spoke with the senior leaders there. The church leaders had been praying and waiting for this very thing and believed this couple's experience was the first fruits of that blessing they had been believing for.

Two nights later this couple sat on their front porch discussing their flower garden, and Geri asked if he had heard one of their friends share a dream about seeing an angel and a feather. As they talked, they looked on with open eyes as an angel flew across the front of the porch and dropped something in the grass below. They ran off the porch to find the second stone, which was clear. As they stood there in awe and bent down to pick it up, Geri began to look around a bit more. Three more stones were hidden in the grass! As it seemed more were appearing, they continued to look and found a red one! They called the church again and told the senior pastors of the five stones that appeared that day.

A few nights later Terry returned home from work again, on a Tuesday. He was collecting his lunch pail and coffee cup and went to the back of the truck to get a larger lunch pail when an angel suddenly appeared there. Both Terry and the angel reached out toward each other when she (the angel) dropped another stone in his outstretched palm and smiled. He turned and yelled for his wife to come out, but when he turned back around to the angel, she was gone, the seventh stone left behind in his hand. After this began to happen, Terry started to have gold dust appear on his clothing when he spoke about God. It has appeared on his food, his clothing, and even in a small pile on the top of his head that was caught on film!

That following Sunday Terry came out to the porch at around eight in the morning, and his son and wife joined him for a while before they left for church. They listened to worship music on a tape and were praising God when two more stones fell. The son didn't see the stones fall, but he saw the look on his father's face and realized more stones had appeared. He leaped over the porch railing to get down to the ground to find what his father had seen fall out of the air and picked up two stones, white and red respectively.

A few days later, Geri was at the house with a friend discussing the stones, and brought the friend out to where the various they had appeared. As they turned around, a pink one fell from the air onto the ground.

One Thursday Terry and his son sat on the porch. They had taken the stones out of the box where they were kept and placed them on a clean cloth when the son noticed there were two pink ones where previously there had only been one! Terry pointed out that it was a trick of the light and it only looked like it was pink—after all, they had a few clear stones. They cleaned the stones with a cloth and placed them in the order they had appeared when Geri came out and pointed out the pink stone was in the wrong place—until she realized there was already a pink one in its appropriate spot. Sometime before they had started cleaning them, the second pink stone had appeared in the box—the eleventh stone! Terry looked at the new pink stone, then counted the stones again. He double and triple checked them until finally his son said, "Dad, no matter how you count them, there are still eleven stones." Sure enough, another miracle had occurred.

The next day the senior pastors came by to borrow two stones to take to a camp meeting as Terry was unable to attend, so Geri brought them out. The stones were kept individually in small containers in a larger box to protect them, but one of the stones was loose inside the box. When she took off the black cloth covering the containers, the container she thought was empty still had a stone in it. The loose stone was extra, which meant now there were twelve!

That Sunday morning during worship at church, the angels dropped a lavender-colored stone, and after the service the couple brought out their gem box to show people the stones, and a new red stone was laying loose in the box.

Shortly after that event, a group came by to interview this couple and record the miracles. During the recording, Terry saw an angel drop the fifteenth stone on their lawn. They didn't catch it appearing on tape, but his reaction was quite genuine when he saw it appear, which is clear in the original video. He noted something peculiar about the angel when it appeared—that it wasn't old, but at the same time was exceedingly ancient, and its clothes were white, but at the same time blue and pink, but not pink and rather white, all at the same time. Much like a pearl changes from color to color when it is turned in the light, there is a shimmering, changing aspect to the appearance and majesty of angels, which further pales in comparison with the glory of God. He hurried down the steps to the grass to pick up the fifteenth stone, which was also pink in color (King).

Forty stones appeared altogether to this couple in what was essentially a complete set, and no more stones appeared to them after that. Prophetically speaking, the number forty represents testing—the forty years the Israelites spent in the desert, Jesus fasting for forty days, and even the rain that fell on the earth for 40 days and nights when Noah and family were in the ark. It could be said that there is an element of judgment or discipline in this testing, but God doesn't test in order to discipline, but rather to reward and bless. I believe this set of gemstones is a prophetic sign to the Body of Christ that God is using this gem manifestation to reveal the deep things in our hearts—to show forth whether it is wood, hay, straw, or precious gems, gold, and silver that are the fruit stored up within us (1 Corinthians 3:12).

Of those forty stones, not all of them are in possession of that couple—a handful of them appeared to other ministers or were given as gifts as the Lord led. On one occasion, a minister couple who have had manna appear from heaven over the course of thirty years visited this couple's house to see where the gems had manifested. During that visit to the property, a radiant lime green stone was dropped from heaven, which the wife now wears in a ring when she ministers.

Having personally seen this stone, it is both large and beautiful, and perfectly matches in size to the other stones of this set that I have seen. The senior pastors of Gateway Church, John and Ruth Filler, are in possession of one of the forty stones, as is another traveling revivalist who focuses on miracles, signs, and wonders—and who has gold dust, gemstones, and other miraculous signs that occur in his meetings as well (Filler).

As an interesting side note, a number of different leaders, including Patricia King of Extreme Prophetic whose ministry was responsible for an in-depth interview chronicling this miracle, noted that Idaho is known as "The Gem State" so it seems a fitting prophetic sign that these gems would appear for a church there (King).

These stones were eventually taken to a series of jewelers to determine authenticity. One professional noted that the gemstones lacked flaws, which is impossible on earth, as all naturally occurring stones have inclusions. Possibly even more interesting is the fact that they lacked the inclusions found in manmade stones as well. If they're not natural gems and not manmade, how many options can there be other than God?

Gemstones Fall in Carolina, Puerto Rico

In Carolina, Puerto Rico, just outside of San Juan, there used to be a church called Casa De Restoracion y de Misericordia (House of Restoration and Mercy). The senior pastor, Pastor Denis Rojas, began pastoring the church in 2003 after he and his wife Pastor Awilda had spent 25 years as evangelists, and on April 22nd of 2004 they obtained a building and gave it its name. The Lord had indicated to them that they should find a house where He could live in and perform miracles, and that God's name would be glorified in many places as a result of the manifestations that He would bring through them. They named the church "House of Restoration and Mercy" as a sign that God would transform, restore, set free, and perform miracles for all who came to the church.

Four months after they started, they invited a woman minister to the church who operated in miracles and who had a Bible that flowed with oil. This woman gave them oil from that Bible and Pastor Awilda, along with seven men in the church, anointed the walls of the church to consecrate it. Two days later, supernatural oil was first observed on an interior glass window just overtop the entrance door to the building— they could see it running down the window pane. They went to the kitchen and found some window cleaning materials to clean the window and the door below it. Two days after that, when they came back to the church again, the door had more oil, but this time both on the inside and outside. It went to the ceiling and on the wall borders, then the stairwell going up to the second floor. After two more weeks it began to saturate into the church and not just the outside of the building. Then, something else spectacular occurred.

A few months after this manifestation began, Pastor Dennis went into a period of prayer and fasting. On the fifth day of that time, God told him to get up and go to the office and look for a camera and to put it on the stand and turn it on to record but stop. At 8:15 in the morning, God said, "In the morning when I tell you to take off the stop, you will see what I do with your Bible." When he took off the stop button and began to record, the Bible immediately began to swell like a sponge and started flowing with oil. The pastor began to shout and cry out. The first time the oil came on the Bible, it had the fragrance of roses, which they believe signified the fragrance of the blood of Jesus. The oil flowed for months, then it stopped for a few weeks. During this time God told them that the oil would change its smell and structure, and after a few weeks it did exactly that (Chung).

The Bible began to shed oil that had the scent of nard, or spikenard. This accounted for the change of smell the Lord had told them about, but something else curious began to occur—the Bible began to drip with a white substance that they first thought was paint, but when they looked closer, it was a brilliant white liquid. A woman in the town of Aguadilla had it analyzed and said it was the extract of nacker from a pearl—the material that pearls are made of. The Lord literally changed the *structure* of the material that flowed out from oil to something else entirely! The church understood this new manifestation to be a message from the Lord signifying the preparation of the minister—God giving them a sign that He was preparing them for His work. They prayed over people and anointed the parishioners with that oil for healing and liberation. The oil stopped for about a month after that until another pastor called the church from Panama with a prophetic word that a new fragrance was coming, and that the fragrance would have a prophetic significance: it would be used to heal. Soon after, the Bible began to flow with the oil of myrrh, signifying the suffering of the physical body (Diaz).

After this happened, gold dust started to fall from the air onto the church members' clothing, hair and even the chairs for a few weeks. The day the dust began to appear, God told Pastor Dennis to dress in black. He asked why, and if there was someone who was going to die. God told him not to question and that God was going to do a miracle. Dennis put on black pants and a black sweater, and he began to pray and go around the church praying for the oil. That night, God told him to stop praying and to go to the altar and worship God's name—to lift up his hands and adore God's name. After half an hour he felt someone had thrown something cold upon him and he got scared. He asked someone to turn on the lights and saw his hands, face, hair, glasses, and all of his clothing were covered with golden colored dust. Everyone was covered with the golden dust that evening. After that, the church members began to get more and more interested in the services for intercession, and more and more people would come to the prayer meetings. After a while, a sapphire-colored dust began to appear, a ruby dust, emerald dust, white diamond, black onyx. The onyx continued for many months before a silver dust began to fall for many more months. They prayed that God would show them who was making this dust fall. One day they came to the church and saw large footprints that showed the toes and heel of the footprint. Each footprint impression in the carpet was 16 inches and filled with color-changing oils.

One Friday a demonized woman came to the church service, moved the chairs that were covering the footprints, and started throwing herself on the footprints. The oil began to burn her skin and the demons started coming out of her; she was liberated from the demons. Two days later, the church had a meeting and God began to speak to Pastor Dennis in his spirit, and instructed him to prophesy that footsteps would appear again. He began to declare that footsteps would appear, and the footstep imprints reappeared. This time they melted into the carpet somehow, but they were 18 inches long (Chung).

Pastor Dennis was in that building for two years with the oil manifestation, but as the church grew in membership, they transferred to another building. They rented and remodeled another space, and about two weeks after they started in the new building, the manifestation of oil began to appear in the new location. When they would adore and praise God, and the people consecrated themselves, the manifestations began to appear on the walls, the oil on the Bible, at times gold dust began to fall, and gemstones started to appear. Sometimes they felt the presence of the Lord moving and some people saw an angel moving in the church (Diaz).

The first gemstone appeared on a Monday during prayer and intercession, months after the myrrh oil had started to flow. They were praying and praising as a large group when God instructed Pastor Dennis to declare to the group that night that He would unleash the sign of the diamonds. He said to the Lord that he was unable to release that because it wasn't in the Bible. God told him that as God, it wasn't the pastor's job to question Him, but only to believe and not to question what God wanted to do and to just declare it anyway. Pastor Dennis began to pray out, "I unleash the anointing of the diamonds and I order now for the skies to open and for the realm of God to come over this house and the manifestation of God over this house and that all diamonds of the kingdom come now and be unleashed."

In that moment, a square diamond fell and hit Pastor Awilda on the back. When she looked on her left thigh, she saw something brilliant. She took it in her hands and couldn't see it very well because the room was dark, so she went to the women's bathroom and turned on the light. When she opened her hand, she saw a color-changing diamond and began to shout out and praise God and cry. The head of the deacons heard her crying in the bathroom and told Pastor Dennis he needed to see why his wife was crying in the bathroom and what was going on. Dennis knocked on the door and asked her what happened. She opened the door, grabbed him and pulled him into the bathroom, then showed him the color-changing diamond that God had given her. He left the bathroom, turned the lights on, and began to show everyone in the congregation. In the bathroom it looked rose-colored, but under the fluorescent lights it appeared purple, but in the morning sun, it would turn white. After this, in all of the following services during prayer and intercession, the gemstones appeared—one or two or five or twenty or more. The pastors noted that the quantity of the stones were linked to the level of adoration of God present in the church at the time.

That was a watershed event for the church because after that the gemstones began to appear—one, two, five, twenty, or more! The pastors noted that the quantity of the stones appeared to be linked to the level of adoration of God present in the church at the time.

At those times, often the angel would leave diamonds behind, which they believe represented how the Lord feels about the church. As of September 22nd, 2007, the church had 1285 gems appear, but by November they had at least 1885 gems that they documented in a register.

When the Bible was left alone on the podium, its pages would always be found turned to the last page of Psalms and first page of Proverbs. This manifestation of oil, gold dust, and gemstones from heaven lasted for over four years. Gem experts shared with the pastors that the quality of the stones depends on the light, cut, and transparency. Per the church's report, some of the gems have been analyzed by jewelers but they have said they are unable to assign a monetary value to the stones because they are cut too perfectly. In August one year, twelve stones appeared, all of which were rectangular-cut, and which looked as though they were the same as the stones in the Ephod found on the High Priest's breastplate in the book of Exodus.

Pastor Dennis believed that because so many people have been saturated with evangelism but still don't believe in Jesus, God is sending miracles to point to the fact that God is real, is present, and He doesn't only have the Bible to uplift our spirits. Instead, God does these miracles so we can know that He is and is alive and uses these miracles to demonstrate His power and authority. The Bible says that we would do greater things in the name of the Lord—things eye has not seen and ear has not heard, that God has reserved in our hearts so that those who believe in Him would experience the manifestation of Heaven coming with evidence to the earth (Chung).

While as of the time of writing this it does not appear that Casa De Restoracion y Misericordia is still a functioning church, the Lord worked many signs, wonders, and miracles for them during the period they were gathered together, and they have helped usher in a new level of faith to the body of Christ to see the Lord manifest His will on the earth in power.

Works Cited

Chung, Pastor Buu Tu. "About Heavenly Oil and Gemstones - An Interview". Online Video Clip. *Youtube*, Youtube. 12 Nov. 2012. Web. 11 June 2016.

Diaz, Alex. "Jewels Falling From Heaven In The Church In Puerto Rico". Online Video Clip. *Youtube*, Youtube. 31 Mar 2010. Web. 12 June 2016.

Fernando, Faustin. "Mission Series | Raining Gemstones in India." Revival Magazine. Revival Magazine, 30 Dec. 2013. Web. 2 July 2015.

Filler, John. Personal interview. 6 Mar. 2016.

King, Patricia. "Gemstones From Heaven." Online Video Clip. XPMedia. Extreme Prophetic. Online Video Clip. 11 Aug. 2006. Web. 11 June 2016.

Mulinde, John. "How Satan Stops Our Prayers!" How Satan Stops Our Prayers, Combat in the Heavenly Realm. Divine Revelations, Nov. 2000. Web. 5 July 2015.

THANK YOU FOR PURCHASING THIS BOOK

Thank you for reading Gemstones From Heaven. This book is the first in a series of books planned to help bring a deeper level of maturity, revelation, and experience to the body about these Last Days signs God is manifesting in the earth. The titles of the books in the **God Signs** series are as follows:

Gemstones from Heaven

Feathers from Heaven

Gold Dust from Heaven

Oil from Heaven

Manna from Heaven

If you enjoyed this book, you can find more free content at www.thekingsofeden.com. Please consider leaving a review on Amazon.com so others can find this book more easily. Feedback is also welcomed by the author at thekingsofeden@gmail.com, and miracle stories such as ones found in this book are always welcome.

Other titles by Michael King include:

The Gamer's Guide to the Kingdom of God

Excerpt from

Feathers From Heaven

Chapter 1

Our Personal Story

"A man with an experience is never at the mercy of an argument."

— Anonymous —

The feathers from heaven began falling for me about ten years ago. The first time I ever saw one appear was in a church I attended while a student in their ministry school. I was at the front of the sanctuary chatting and praying for some people when I saw a tiny wisp of a feather appear in midair at around head height. We all watched as it floated slowly upwards, and then, as if by some trick of the light, the feather became hard to see and then disappeared altogether.

I had heard of this phenomenon before but had never seen it. The miracle was pretty astounding.

The second time I found a feather from heaven was after I drove home from visiting a friend, who I am pleased to say is now my wife. She had some pretty intense spiritual activity going on at her house, and feathers, gold dust, and oil were appearing supernaturally with some level of frequency. At any rate, I got in the car and drove home at the end of a night of worship and prayer. As I got out of the car and looked back into the vehicle, a small brown and black feather was on the seat where I had been sitting! I lived in a city at the time and there weren't any birds hanging around that would have conveniently deposited colored feathers inside the car, especially since there was no feather present when I first sat down! I remembered that when I first got in the car I had made a comment about an angel I had just perceived and had looked at the seat before sitting down. Interestingly enough the angel's name was Herald and I suspect he was the one who had left the feather. I kept it in my Bible for years after that.

A number of years later, in 2009, I felt the Lord impress upon me to call a prayer meeting on the day of Pentecost. Only myself, my wife, and a friend showed up, but we all got touched by Holy Spirit. For the next week after I saw a feather float by at some point almost every day—once on the elevator at work, another few times randomly at home, and if I remember correctly, one appeared in my car! All of these were the tiny white wisps, but it was super encouraging to me to see visible fruit for what I had been praying and believing for—namely signs, wonders, and miracles.

Since then I have seen so many feathers I can't even remember half of the times they have appeared. Sometimes it is when we are praying or doing something overtly spiritual; other times they just appear at random with no sort of special preparation or obvious spiritual precursor. One example of this is a day after my wife and I had been at a Christian conference in the area. We were cuddling on our bed streaming a TV show on our laptop when during the show a feather gently floated across the screen. I lightly pincered it between my thumb and forefinger then opened them to look at it. The feather was gone, but in its place, my fingertips were covered in golden sparkly dust. This dust quickly spread to cover that hand. I looked at the other hand and suddenly it was covered too. My wife held out her hands and they, too, were instantly covered. It finally stopped spreading when both of our arms up to the shoulders were covered in this fine, sparkly, beautiful golden dust. I can't say I understood some deep purpose for that encounter, but it was certainly a nice surprise!

A few years ago I was a nurse case manager at an assisted living facility. I was talking to another nurse, one of my coworkers, about some of the miracles God was doing in our midst, and at that very moment, a feather appeared in midair and floated there. He was pretty astounded. Another nurse entered the office and he immediately started telling her all about it. It was so fun for me to hear him talk because his excitement was genuine. This other nurse wasn't sure about it and asked him if he was trying to fool her. "Oh my God no, I swear on the Holy Bible it's true!" he said with excitement. That comment still makes me smile to this day. There is something about the first time someone experiences a miracle that is so precious and real—the emotions are brutally honest, hard to hide, and the shock and excitement is such a joy to witness. The realness in someone comes to the surface because they aren't hiding behind the masks we so often wear.

When I had just started to work on this book, my wife and I had the blessing of spending all afternoon and evening with a dear friend who was ordained by Ruth Ward Heflin. We spent hours discussing gold dust, gemstones, and hearing her share her own wonderful glory realm stories and memories with Ruth at the Campmeeting in Ashland, Virginia. It was a fantastically glorious time, and my heart was soaring. Late in the evening we prayed for my wife as she had been dealing with some health issues. As we began to break witchcraft off her, I had my eyes closed in prayer. When I opened them and looked down, a feather that was about two inches long had appeared on my arm and caught me totally by surprise. The angels were hard at work warring on her behalf! My wife was ecstatic and said, "They came for me!" She reported that her head felt better after the fact as well.

A few months later, we made some new friends in Coeur D'Alene, Idaho and met the senior pastors of Gateway Christian Fellowship who had their own exciting feather stories that they graciously shared with us, found in Chapter 7. I took some pictures of the feather in their story and was blessed to be able to use it as the cover picture for this book. Yes, the feather on the cover is a real feather from heaven! Not only that, but toward the end of that weekend, we had feathers appear in our hotel room after we had spent much of that time discussing the glory realm and signs, wonders, and miracles.

Feathers continue to appear on an ongoing basis— sometimes more frequent than others, but each time I am reminded of the Father's love for me, the angelic protection that is around me, and that I am surrounded by a realm that is both unseen and highly active in my life. There is something special about this manifestation, both simple and elegant. It has the ability to turn our focus toward God at a moment's notice, interrupting the daily doldrums with the breath of heaven. It is my hope that this book—the divine revelation, our stories, and the stories of others—will open this arena of miracles, angelic visitations, and the glory realm of heaven for every reader, and that they, too, would experience and see an increase in the manifestation of feathers from heaven.

About the Author

Michael King is a prolific writer by day and a Registered Nurse by night. He hungrily explores all things spiritual and his love for God has given him a passion for signs, wonders, and miracles. Michael is married to a beautiful wife who doubles as his professional editor. He is known by family and friends for his proficiency in the prophetic and in healing prayer and energy work. His blog, thekingsofeden.com, focuses on spirituality with a hint of health-related topics along with a dash of his fiction and fantasy writing. He is available for speaking engagements on request.

CPSIA information can be obtained at www.ICGtesting.com
Printed in the USA
LVOW07s2007250916

506141LV00002B/497/P